GREAT POWER COMPETITION: IMPLICATIONS FOR DEFENSE

ISSUES FOR CONGRESS

CONGRESSIONAL RESEARCH SERVICE

NIMBLE BOOKS LLC: THE AI LAB FOR BOOK-LOVERS

FRED ZIMMERMAN, EDITOR

Humans and AI making books richer, more diverse, and more surprising.

PUBLISHING INFORMATION

(c) 2023 Nimble Books LLC
ISBN: 978-1-60888-260-1

AI-GENERATED KEYWORD PHRASES

great power competition; strategic competition; U.S. defense issues; grand strategy; force-planning standards; organizational changes; Department of Defense; nuclear weapons; deterrence; global military posture; military capabilities; Indo-Pacific region; Europe; operational concepts; high-end conventional warfare; U.S. superiority; conventional weapon technologies; innovation; weapon system development; deployment; mobilization capabilities; supply chain security; countering hybrid warfare; gray-zone tactics; Congress; defense planning; budgeting; Biden Administration;

FRONT MATTER

Publishing Information ii

AI-generated Keyword Phrases ii

Abstracts...iii

    TL;DR (one word) iii

    Explain It To Me Like I'm Five Years Old.....................iii

    TL;DR (vanilla)..iv

    Scientific Style iv

    Action Items..v

Viewpoints vi

    Grounds for Dissent..vi

    Red Team Critique vii

    MAGA Perspective...ix

    Implications for Space Force...................................x

    Implications for Enlisted Guardians...........................xi

Page-by-Page Summaries xiii

Notable Passages...xviii

The Space Power Series and Space Sentinel xxiv

ABSTRACTS

TL;DR (ONE WORD)

Competition

EXPLAIN IT TO ME LIKE I'M FIVE YEARS OLD

This document talks about how the United States is in competition with China and Russia, which are big countries. This competition affects the defense, which means the things the US does to protect itself. The document talks about different things that are important for the US defense, like planning, weapons, and how the military is organized. It also talks about how the US wants to be better than other countries in terms of weapons and technology. It says that the US government and Congress, which is a group of important

TL;DR (VANILLA)

This document discusses the implications of increased competition between the United States and China and Russia on U.S. defense issues. It covers various aspects such as grand strategy, force planning, organizational changes, nuclear weapons, military capabilities in different regions, innovation in weapon systems, supply chain security, and countering hybrid warfare. The document emphasizes the role of Congress in determining defense planning and budgeting. It also discusses the concept of Great Power Competition (GPC) and its implications for defense. The Biden Administration's National Security Strategy identifies major challenges from China and Russia and highlights the need for the United States to modernize its military to compete effectively.

SCIENTIFIC STYLE

This document examines the implications of increased competition between the United States and China and Russia, known as great power competition (GPC), on U.S. defense issues. It discusses various aspects that are currently being discussed in relation to U.S. defense, including grand strategy, force planning, organizational changes within the Department of Defense, nuclear weapons and deterrence, global military presence, military capabilities in specific regions, operational concepts, conventional warfare, technological superiority, innovation, mobilization capabilities, supply chain security, and countering hybrid warfare tactics. The document emphasizes the role of Congress in determining how U.S. defense planning and funding should respond to GPC and highlights the importance of the Biden Administration's defense strategy and proposed funding levels. It also explores the concept of Great Power Competition and its implications for defense, highlighting its recognition in the strategies of previous administrations. The document emphasizes the need for the United States to modernize and strengthen its military in order to compete with major powers and address shared challenges.

ACTION ITEMS

Review and analyze the implications of intensified competition between the United States, China, and Russia on U.S. defense issues.

Assess the impact of great power competition on various elements of U.S. defense, such as grand strategy, force-planning standards, organizational changes, nuclear weapons and deterrence, global military posture, military capabilities in specific regions, operational concepts, conventional warfare, weapon technologies, innovation, mobilization capabilities, supply chain security, and countering hybrid warfare and gray-zone tactics.

Evaluate the role of Congress in determining U.S. defense planning and budgeting in response to great power conflict.

VIEWPOINTS

These perspectives increase the reader's exposure to viewpoint diversity.

GROUNDS FOR DISSENT

Non-interventionist Perspective: A member of the organization might dissent from this report based on a principled belief in non-interventionism or isolationism. They may argue that intensified competition between the United States and other countries is unnecessary and potentially harmful to global stability. They could believe that focusing on military capabilities and grand strategies only serves to escalate tensions and provoke conflicts. Instead, they might advocate for a more diplomatic approach, emphasizing cooperation and dialogue with other nations to address global challenges.

Cost and Resource Allocation: Another reason for dissent could be rooted in concerns over the allocation of resources. The member might argue that the document places too much emphasis on defense spending and military capabilities, leading to an imbalance in government budget priorities. They could contend that excessive military spending diverts funds from critical domestic needs such as healthcare, education, infrastructure, or social welfare programs. This perspective may prioritize investing in civilian sectors rather than maintaining a robust military presence.

Focus on Domestic Issues: A dissenting member might believe that the document overlooks pressing domestic issues that require attention and resources. They might argue that the United States should prioritize addressing income inequality, racial injustice, climate change, or healthcare access over preparing for great power competition. This perspective sees a disconnect between allocating significant resources to international military competition while neglecting internal challenges that impact the well-being of American citizens.

Multilateral Cooperation: Some members might dissent due to a belief in the importance of multilateralism and collaboration with other nations. They could argue that the document's focus on competition perpetuates a zero-sum mindset, hindering opportunities for mutually beneficial cooperation. They might advocate for strengthening international institutions and fostering closer relationships with China, Russia, and other major powers to find common ground and tackle shared global issues collectively.

Ethical Concerns: A member might dissent based on ethical considerations. They may object to the document's acknowledgment of nuclear weapons, arguing that the focus should be on disarmament and non-proliferation rather than maintaining and modernizing an arsenal. They might also have reservations about the potential human cost of high-end conventional warfare or gray-zone tactics, advocating for a more peaceful approach to resolving conflicts.

It is important to note that these dissenting views are hypothetical and do not represent any specific individual or organization's actual stance. The reasons provided are intended to showcase a range of possible principled and substantive objections that someone within the organization might have to this report.

RED TEAM CRITIQUE

The document provides a comprehensive overview of the implications of intensified competition between the United States and China and Russia on defense issues. It covers a wide range of topics including grand strategy, force-planning standards, organizational changes within the Department of Defense, nuclear weapons and deterrence, global military posture, military capabilities in specific regions, new operational concepts, high-end conventional warfare, technological superiority, innovation, mobilization capabilities, supply chain security, and countering hybrid warfare and gray-zone tactics.

Overall, the document does a good job of identifying key areas that need to be addressed in response to great power competition. However, there are several areas where the document could benefit from further analysis and critique.

First, while the document mentions the acknowledgment of great power competition in the strategies of the Obama, Trump, and Biden administrations, it fails to provide a critical assessment of the effectiveness of these strategies. Were they successful in effectively countering the challenges posed by China and Russia? What were the strengths and weaknesses of each administration's approach? Without this analysis, it is difficult to determine the best path forward.

Second, the document emphasizes the need for the United States to modernize and strengthen its military to compete with major powers. However, it does not adequately address the potential risks and unintended consequences of such a strategy. For example, what are the potential escalatory risks of increasing military capabilities in the Indo-Pacific region and Europe? How might this affect arms races and instability in these regions?

In addition, the document briefly mentions the importance of maintaining U.S. superiority in conventional weapon technologies but does not delve into specifics. What specific technologies or capabilities are crucial for maintaining this superiority? How does the U.S. compare to China and Russia in these areas? A more detailed analysis of these issues would provide a clearer understanding of the challenges and opportunities for the U.S. defense industrial base.

Lastly, the document acknowledges the role of Congress in determining defense planning and budgeting, but it does not thoroughly explore the potential obstacles and political dynamics that may hinder the implementation of the Biden Administration's defense strategy. How might partisan politics and competing interests shape the decision-making process? What are the challenges of securing funding for defense priorities in an era of fiscal constraints?

In conclusion, while the document provides a strong foundation for understanding the implications of great power competition on U.S. defense issues, it would benefit from further analysis and critique in some areas. A more critical assessment of past strategies, a deeper exploration of potential risks and unintended consequences, a detailed analysis of technological superiority, and an examination of political dynamics would enhance the document's overall effectiveness.

MAGA PERSPECTIVE

This document is just another example of the Biden administration's obsession with so-called "great power competition" and their misplaced priorities. Instead of focusing on issues that actually matter to the American people, like jobs and immigration, they are wasting time and resources on military posturing against China and Russia.

The notion that we need to "strengthen our military" to compete with these countries is laughable. The United States already has the most powerful military in the world by far. We spend more on defense than the next ten countries combined. How much stronger do we need to be?

Furthermore, this document conveniently ignores the fact that China and Russia are not our biggest threats. The real danger comes from within, with radical leftists trying to undermine our Constitution and destroy America from the inside. Instead of worrying about imaginary threats abroad, we should be focusing on securing our borders and protecting our freedoms at home.

The mention of Congress playing a role in determining defense planning and budgeting is a joke. Congress has repeatedly shown that they are more interested in political grandstanding than actually supporting our military. They cut funding for vital defense programs while virtue signaling to their base. It's clear that they care more about their own reelection campaigns than the safety of our nation.

Lastly, the emphasis on countering so-called "hybrid warfare" and "gray-zone tactics" is just another excuse for the government to infringe on our civil liberties. We don't need to give the government more power and control in the name of national security. Our founding fathers warned us about the dangers of a bloated military-industrial complex, and it's clear that their warnings still hold true today.

IMPLICATIONS FOR SPACE FORCE

BY SPACE SENTINEL, THE AUTHORITATIVE GPT GUIDE ON SPACE, NATIONAL SECURITY, AND SPACE INDUSTRIALIZATION.

The Congressional Research Service report "Great Power Competition: Implications for Defense—Issues for Congress" (Updated October 3, 2023) presents a comprehensive overview of the strategic shift in U.S. defense and security priorities in the context of intensified competition with China and Russia. This shift has profound implications for the U.S. Space Force and its doctrine, particularly in areas related to grand strategy and geopolitics, force-planning standards, organizational changes within the Department of Defense, and nuclear weapons and deterrence.

1. **Grand Strategy and Geopolitics**: The report underscores a renewed emphasis on grand strategy and geopolitics as a starting point for U.S. defense issues. For the Space Force, this translates into a strategic focus on space as a domain of great power rivalry, especially considering the increasing space capabilities of China and Russia. The Space Force is tasked with ensuring U.S. superiority and freedom of operation in space, which is pivotal in the context of great power competition.

2. **Force-Planning Standard**: The document discusses the force-planning standard, i.e., the size and capability of the U.S. military to handle conflicts. Given the rising space capabilities of adversaries, the Space Force must be adequately sized and equipped to handle potential space-related conflicts or contingencies. This might involve expanding its capabilities and resources to address multiple, simultaneous space threats.

3. **Organizational Changes within DOD**: The emergence of great power competition has led to organizational changes within the DOD. The creation of the U.S. Space Force itself is a significant organizational change, representing a recognition of the increasing importance of space in national security and defense strategy. The Space Force's doctrine must align with these changes to effectively counter strategic competitors in space.

4. **Nuclear Weapons, Nuclear Deterrence, and Arms Control**: The report highlights the renewed focus on nuclear deterrence and arms control, especially concerning China and Russia. The Space Force plays a critical role in this aspect, as space capabilities are integral to the U.S.'s nuclear command, control, and communications systems. Ensuring the security and resilience of these space-based assets is crucial for effective nuclear deterrence.

The Space Force, as a critical component of U.S. defense strategy, must adapt its doctrine and capabilities to address these evolving strategic dynamics. Its role in ensuring space superiority, protecting U.S. assets in space, and supporting overall national security objectives in the face of great power competition is more crucial than ever.

IMPLICATIONS FOR ENLISTED GUARDIANS

ALSO BY SPACE SENTINEL

For an enlisted Guardian specializing in space domain awareness (SDA), the insights from the Congressional Research Service report on Great Power Competition have several direct implications:

1. **Enhanced Focus on Space as a Strategic Domain**: The intensified competition with China and Russia necessitates a heightened focus on space as a battleground for strategic advantage. Enlisted Guardians in SDA roles must be acutely aware of the increased activities of adversarial nations in space. This includes monitoring satellite deployments, space debris, and potential anti-satellite (ASAT) capabilities of these nations.

2. **Increased Importance of Space Surveillance and Reconnaissance**: The report's emphasis on grand strategy and geopolitics translates into the need for robust space surveillance. Enlisted Guardians must be adept at using space surveillance technologies to detect, track, and catalog objects in space, ensuring the U.S. has a comprehensive understanding of the space environment and any potential threats.

3. **Adaptation to New Organizational Structures and Doctrines**: Organizational changes within the DOD, including the establishment of the Space Force, require enlisted personnel to adapt to new doctrines and

operational strategies. This means staying informed about evolving space doctrines and integrating these principles into daily SDA operations.

4. **Supporting Nuclear Deterrence through Space Domain Awareness**: Given the renewed focus on nuclear deterrence and arms control, enlisted Guardians in SDA play a crucial role in supporting these efforts. Effective SDA ensures the integrity of satellite networks crucial for nuclear command and control communications. Guardians must be vigilant in monitoring any activities that could threaten these critical space assets.

5. **Preparedness for Multi-Domain Operations**: The shift in force-planning standards towards addressing the capabilities of major powers like China and Russia means that enlisted Guardians must be prepared for operations that may span multiple domains (air, land, sea, cyber, and space). This requires an understanding of how actions in space impact other domains and vice versa.

6. **Emphasis on Collaboration and Intelligence Sharing**: The evolving nature of space threats necessitates collaboration within the U.S. military branches and with allied nations. Enlisted Guardians must be proficient in intelligence sharing and joint operations, understanding the global nature of space domain challenges.

In summary, an enlisted Guardian in the space domain awareness field must be highly skilled in surveillance and reconnaissance, adaptable to changing strategic doctrines, and cognizant of the broader geopolitical landscape. Their role is critical in maintaining U.S. strategic advantages in space, a domain increasingly central to national security in the context of great power competition.

PAGE-BY-PAGE SUMMARIES

0   *N/A*

1   *The emergence of great power competition with China and Russia has shifted the focus of US defense issues. Congress must decide how to respond and whether to approve the Biden Administration's proposed defense strategy and funding levels, which could impact US defense capabilities and the defense industrial base.*

2   *This page provides an overview of the implications of great power competition for defense, including changes in strategy, force planning, nuclear weapons, military posture, and capabilities. It also highlights issues for Congress to consider.*

3   *This report discusses the implications of intensified competition between the US, China, and Russia for US defense. It explores how Congress should respond to this competition and its impact on defense capabilities and funding requirements. The report does not address implications for other policy areas.*

4   *The page discusses the shift in U.S. national security strategy towards a focus on Great Power Competition (GPC), as acknowledged by the Obama and Trump administrations. The Biden administration's National Security Strategy highlights the end of the post-Cold War era and the competition between major powers, particularly China and Russia, while also addressing shared global challenges.*

5   *The page discusses the challenges posed by Russia and China to the international order. It highlights Russia's immediate threat through aggression and destabilization, while China aims to reshape the international order with its growing power. The United States plans to modernize its military to compete with major powers. The National Security Strategy emphasizes the need to outcompete China and constrain Russia.*

6   *The page discusses the Biden Administration's National Defense Strategy, which focuses on strengthening deterrence against China and Russia. It emphasizes collaboration with allies and partners, preventing dominance by China, and dissuading aggression. The strategy also acknowledges the threat posed by Russia and other persistent threats such as North Korea and Iran.*

7   *The page discusses the growing threat posed by China and Russia to US interests and global stability. It highlights China's expansion and modernization of its military capabilities, including space, cyber, and nuclear capabilities. It also mentions Russia's territorial aggression and various threats it poses, such as nuclear, cyber, and undersea warfare. The US aims to bolster deterrence and enhance its technological edge through collaboration with allies and partners.*

8   *The page discusses the implications of great power competition, particularly with China and Russia, for US defense. It highlights the shift in focus from counterterrorism to geopolitical concerns and the need for a resilient joint force.*

9   *The resurgence of Russia and rise of China necessitates a solid grand strategy for the US, focused on preventing regional hegemons in Eurasia. This strategy guides the structure and capabilities of the US military. However, it is not set in stone and may need reevaluation in light of changing circumstances.*

10   *The emergence of Great Power Competition (GPC) prompts discussion on U.S. grand strategy and force-planning standards. The U.S. military is currently sized to handle one major conflict, not two simultaneous conflicts. The two-war strategy has eroded due to budget cuts and the rise of major power adversaries.*

11   *The page discusses the shift in the US military's force-planning construct towards preparing for high-intensity conflicts with great-power adversaries like China and*

Russia. It explores the debate over adopting a two-war standard and potential organizational changes within the Department of Defense to counter these threats.

12   The page discusses the implications of great power competition on defense, particularly in relation to nuclear weapons and deterrence. It highlights Russia and China's nuclear capabilities and the need for the US to consider adjustments to its nuclear strategy.

13   The page discusses the implications of great power competition, particularly in the context of nuclear weapons and deterrence. It highlights the need for modernization of US strategic nuclear deterrent forces and the challenges posed by the emergence of a three-power strategic nuclear situation.

14   The page discusses the growing nuclear capabilities and threats posed by China and Russia. It highlights the need for the United States to take steps to reduce the role of nuclear weapons and pursue arms control to strengthen deterrence and non-proliferation efforts. The invasion of Ukraine by Russia serves as a reminder of the risks and dangers associated with nuclear conflict.

15   The page discusses the implications of great power competition, particularly in relation to nuclear weapons, and the need for deterrence strategies against Russia and China. It also mentions the debate over the development of a new nuclear-armed sea-launched cruise missile and the role of arms control in this context.

16   The page discusses the potential for arms control talks between the United States and China, highlighting China's reluctance to engage in negotiations unless the US reduces its nuclear forces. The White House has emphasized that these discussions are not at the same level as those with Russia.

17   The page discusses the Biden administration's decision to cut off arms control talks with Russia and China's lack of interest in discussing nuclear weapons reduction. It also mentions the need for guardrails in the US-China relationship and concerns about China's lack of transparency regarding its nuclear build-up. Additionally, it highlights the increased discussion about global US military posture in response to the emergence of great power competition.

18   The page discusses the ongoing debate about the regional distribution of U.S. military capabilities and force deployments, particularly in relation to countering China's growing military capabilities in the Indo-Pacific region and addressing security challenges posed by Russia in Europe and the Middle East. Key issues include prioritizing defense planning for Europe versus the Indo-Pacific, the influence of Russia's invasion of Ukraine on China's actions towards Taiwan, and potential changes in U.S. grand strategy, defense strategy, and defense budget.

19   The page discusses the Obama and Trump administrations' efforts to shift U.S. military forces to the Asia-Pacific region to counter China, and the potential risks of reducing force deployments in other regions.

20   The Biden Administration is conducting a Global Posture Review to align military forces with foreign policy priorities. The review will consider the location of service members, including rotational forces in Poland and Korea, as well as naval forces. The Indo-Pacific region is a priority, reflecting the focus on China as a challenge. The review is expected to be completed by mid-year.

21   The global posture review aims to strengthen U.S. deterrence against China and Russia while supporting counterterrorism efforts. Specific initiatives include enhancing infrastructure in Guam and Australia, increasing military partnership activities, and realigning forces in Europe, the Middle East, Africa, and Central/South America. Details of the review are classified.

22   *The page discusses the implications of great power competition for defense and the issues facing Congress. It highlights the impact of Russia's invasion of Ukraine on U.S. defense planning in the Indo-Pacific region and the complications arising from developments in the Middle East. The need for potential changes in U.S. grand strategy, defense strategy, and defense budget is also mentioned.*

23   *The page discusses the withdrawal of certain U.S. forces from the Middle East to be redeployed elsewhere, as well as the focus on strengthening U.S. military capabilities in the Indo-Pacific region to counter China. It mentions the Free and Open Indo-Pacific policy and the priorities outlined in the 2022 National Defense Strategy.*

24   *The page discusses the implications of great power competition for defense and highlights potential measures to counter China in the Indo-Pacific region, including shifting to distributed force architectures, utilizing unmanned vehicles, increasing longer-ranged aircraft and missiles, and enhancing C4ISR capabilities. The Navy has already taken actions to strengthen military capabilities in the region.*

25   *The page discusses the importance of strengthening US military capabilities in the Indo-Pacific region, particularly in response to China's growing influence. It mentions the Pacific Deterrence Initiative (PDI) as a collection of investments aimed at bolstering military capabilities in the region.*

26   *The page discusses the strengthening of U.S. military force deployments in the Indo-Pacific region and the need to enhance U.S. and NATO capabilities in Europe to counter potential Russian aggression. Measures include increasing military presence in countries like Poland and improving combat power and critical enablers.*

27   *The page discusses the implications of great power competition for defense and highlights the U.S. military's focus on new operational concepts and capabilities for high-end conventional warfare. It also mentions the U.S. Navy's actions in European waters and NATO's efforts to increase defense spending.*

28   *The page discusses the implications of great power competition for defense and highlights the shift in focus towards high-end conventional warfare. It mentions various weapon acquisition programs and capabilities that have been prioritized as a result of this emphasis.*

29   *The page discusses the implications of great power competition for defense and highlights the need for the US to maintain superiority in conventional weapon technologies. It also mentions the role of special operations forces in supporting the national defense strategy.*

30   *The page discusses the Biden Administration's focus on making technology investments to maintain the United States' military advantage. It mentions specific areas of technological development, such as directed energy, hypersonics, cyber, and biotechnology. The Department of Defense is also developing a strategy for investment in critical technology areas to stay ahead of adversaries.*

31   *The US Department of Defense is prioritizing innovation and speed in weapon system development to quickly incorporate new technologies. The military services are taking actions to increase innovation, including the use of special acquisition authorities. A new defense acquisition framework has been introduced to accelerate the process of developing and fielding new weapons.*

32   *DOD needs to prioritize innovation and speed in response to Great Power Competition (GPC) but must also address reliability issues and adjust acquisition policy to emphasize time as a risk factor. Some argue that DOD is not moving quickly enough, while others advocate for more experimentation and tolerance of failure.*

33   *The page discusses the increased emphasis on U.S. mobilization capabilities for extended-length conflicts in the context of great power competition. Concerns have been raised about the adequacy of these capabilities and recommendations have been made to improve them.*

34   *Concerns over U.S. industrial mobilization capabilities have been reinforced by the finite inventories of weapons and equipment, as well as limits on industrial capacity, highlighted by the response to Russia's invasion of Ukraine.*

35   *The page discusses the need for improved mobilization capabilities in the US military, including the use of machine learning and artificial intelligence. It also highlights the importance of supply chain security and reducing reliance on components from China and Russia.*

36   *The page discusses the implications of great power competition for defense and highlights concerns about supply chain security and countering hybrid warfare tactics employed by Russia and China. The Biden Administration has taken steps to improve supply chain resilience and address these challenges.*

37   *The page discusses the implications of great power competition for defense and highlights potential policy and oversight issues for Congress, including the accuracy of the Biden Administration's national security strategy and the force-planning standard being used.*

38   *The page discusses various issues for Congress to consider regarding the implications of great power competition, including conflicts with China and Russia, DOD organization, nuclear weapons, U.S. military posture, capabilities in the Indo-Pacific region and Europe, new operational concepts, high-end conventional warfare, and maintaining U.S. superiority in conventional weapon technologies.*

39   *The page discusses key issues for Congress regarding defense in the context of great power competition. These include innovation and speed in weapon system development, mobilization capabilities, supply chain security, and countering hybrid warfare tactics.*

40   *The page discusses the transition from the post-Cold War era to the current era of Great Power Competition (GPC). It provides background information on the Cold War era, the post-Cold War era, and the emergence of GPC.*

41   *Great power competition has replaced the post-Cold War era, with the United States, China, and Russia engaged in renewed ideological, technological, and military competition. This shift is marked by Russia's annexation of Crimea in 2014 and challenges to the U.S.-led international order. Other factors include regional security challenges, countering terrorism, and weak or failed states.*

42   *The page discusses markers of the shift from the post-Cold War era to Great Power Competition (GPC), including declines in freedom, Putin's speech on a multipolar order, Russia's invasion of Georgia, and China's economic success and assertive actions.*

43   *The page discusses the comparisons made between the current situation of Great Power Competition (GPC) and past international security environments such as the Cold War and the multipolar situation before World War I. It highlights the differences and similarities between these situations and emphasizes the need for direct observation to understand the key features of the current GPC.*

44   *The page discusses the current situation of great power competition and its implications for defense. It also highlights the previous shift from the Cold War to the post-Cold War era and the changes it brought to defense funding, strategy, and missions.*

45   *This page provides a list of articles about the transition to Great Power Competition (GPC) and GPC in general, including discussions on the return of geopolitics and the challenges faced by the United States in a changing international system.*

48 This page contains a list of citations from various sources discussing the implications of great power competition and the changing world order.

49 This page contains a list of citations from various sources discussing the implications of great power competition and the changing international order, particularly in relation to Russia and China.

53 Various articles discuss the implications of the war in Ukraine on global power dynamics, highlighting the potential for a more dangerous world order and the shifting geopolitical landscape.

55 This page provides a list of articles discussing grand strategy and geopolitics for the United States in the context of Great Power Competition.

58 This page provides a list of citations from various sources discussing the implications of great power competition for defense and issues for Congress.

70 A list of articles and reports discussing the implications of great power competition and the need for elevated American foreign policy in response.

71 This page provides a list of readings on supply chain security, including executive branch documents, congressional reports, and GAO reports.

73 Press reports and readings highlight concerns about the US military's reliance on Chinese-made equipment, potential supply chain vulnerabilities, and the need to reshore the defense department's supply chain.

74 N/A

75 This page provides a list of articles discussing the implications and challenges of great power competition on defense supply chains, including issues with foreign dependencies, critical minerals supply chains, Chinese money in the US defense industry, and the need for supply chain resilience.

76 N/A

77 This page provides citations to articles discussing Russian and Chinese irregular, hybrid, and gray-zone warfare tactics and possible U.S. strategies for countering those tactics.

83 This page contains a list of articles and reports discussing the implications and challenges of great power competition, particularly in the gray zone, for defense and national security.

84 N/A

85 The page discusses the implications of great power competition for defense and highlights the need for reevaluating irregular warfare and information operations.

86 This page discusses the role of Congress in responding to the transition from the Cold War to the post-Cold War era in the late 1980s and early 1990s. It highlights the significant role played by Congress in reassessing defense funding levels, strategy, plans, and programs during this period.

Notable Passages

1   The emergence over the past decade of intensified U.S. competition with the People's Republic of China (PRC or China) and the Russian Federation (Russia)—often referred to as great power competition (GPC) or strategic competition—has profoundly changed the conversation about U.S. defense issues from what it was during the post–Cold War era: Counterterrorist operations and U.S. military operations in the Middle East—which had been more at the center of discussions of U.S. defense issues following the terrorist attacks of September 11, 2001—are now a less-prominent element in the conversation, and the conversation now focuses more on the following elements, all of which relate largely to China and/or Russia.

3   "For some observers, the ending of the post–Cold War era and emergence of GPC has been underscored by China and Russia's announced strategic partnership and by Russia's invasion of multiple parts of Ukraine starting on February 24, 2022."

4   "The basic laws and principles governing relations among nations, including the United Nations Charter and the protection it affords all states from being invaded by their neighbors or having their borders redrawn by force, are under attack. The risk of conflict between major powers is increasing" (p. 7).

5   "The PRC is the only competitor with both the intent to reshape the international order and, increasingly, the economic, diplomatic, military, and technological power to do it. Beijing has ambitions to create an enhanced sphere of influence in the Indo-Pacific and to become the world's leading power. It is using its technological capacity and increasing influence over international institutions to create more permissive conditions for its own authoritarian model, and to mold global technology use and norms to privilege its interests and values" (p. 23).

6   "The most comprehensive and serious challenge to U.S. national security is the PRC's coercive and increasingly aggressive endeavor to refashion the Indo-Pacific region and the international system to suit its interests and authoritarian preferences. The PRC seeks to undermine U.S. alliances and security partnerships in the Indo-Pacific region, and leverage its growing capabilities, including its economic influence and the People's Liberation Army's (PLA)9 growing strength and military footprint ..."

7   "The PRC's increasingly provocative rhetoric and coercive activity towards Taiwan are destabilizing, risk miscalculation, and threaten the peace and stability of the Taiwan Strait. This is part of a broader pattern of destabilizing and coercive PRC behavior that stretches across the East China Sea, the South China Sea, and along the Line of Actual Control [between China and India]. The PRC has expanded and modernized nearly every aspect of the PLA, with a focus on offsetting U.S. military advantages. The PRC is therefore the pacing challenge for the Department."

8   The emergence of GPC has profoundly changed the conversation about U.S. defense issues from what it was during the post–Cold War era: Counterterrorist operations and U.S. military operations in the Middle East—which had been more at the center of discussions of U.S. defense issues following the terrorist attacks of September 11, 2001— are now a less-prominent element in the conversation, and the conversation now focuses

more on the topics discussed briefly in the sections below, all of which relate largely to China and/or Russia.

9 *"The era of everything [i.e., multiple international security challenges] is the era of grand strategy," Work said, suggesting that the United States must carefully marshal and deploy its great yet limited resources.*

10 *"After the onset of budgetary austerity in 2011, the two-war strategy gradually eroded as defense cuts made it harder to handle two regional adversaries at once. And after the Russian invasion of Ukraine in 2014, it was clear that the U.S. was facing a fundamentally different world, in which the country's foremost adversaries were not inferior rogue states but major powers fielding formidable military capabilities. Add in that any war against Russia or China is likely to occur in their geopolitical backyards, and that both rivals have spent considerable time, money and intellectual effort seeking to neutralize America's ability to project power, and the U.S. military would have enormous difficulty in winning even a single war against a great-power challenger."*

11 *"In the 2018 National Defense Strategy and subsequent statements, the Pentagon thus outlined a significantly different force-planning construct. It announced that the fully mobilized American military would be capable of defeating aggression by a great-power adversary, while also deterring (not necessarily defeating) aggression in a second theater. In other words, the U.S. is now building a force not around the demands of two regional conflicts with rogue states, but around the requirements of winning a high-intensity conflict with a single, top-tier competitor—a war with China over Taiwan, for instance, or a clash with Russia in the Baltic region."*

12 *By the 2030s the United States will, for the first time in its history, face two major nuclear powers as strategic competitors and potential adversaries. This will create new stresses on stability and new challenges for deterrence, assurance, arms control, and risk reduction.... The PRC's nuclear expansion and the changes this could bring to its strategy present new complexities. In the near-term, we must factor this into our arms control and risk reduction approaches with Russia. We also recognize that as the security environment evolves, it may be necessary to consider nuclear strategy and force adjustments to assure our ability to achieve deterrence and other objectives for the PRC – even as we continue to.*

13 *"To ensure our nuclear deterrent remains responsive to the threats we face, we are modernizing the nuclear Triad, nuclear command, control, and communications, and our nuclear weapons infrastructure, as well as strengthening our extended deterrence commitments to our Allies."*

14 *"By the 2030s the United States will, for the first time in its history, face two major nuclear powers as strategic competitors and potential adversaries. This will create new stresses on stability and new challenges for deterrence, assurance, arms control, and risk reduction."*

15 *"The current and growing salience of nuclear weapons in the strategies and forces of our competitors heightens the risks associated with strategic competition and the stakes of crisis and military confrontation. As the NDS notes, we must be able to deter conventional aggression that has the potential to escalate to nuclear employment of any scale. Russia presents the most acute example of this problem today given its significantly larger stockpile of regional nuclear systems and the possibility it would use these forces to try to win a war on its periphery or avoid defeat if it was in danger of losing a conventional war. Deterring Russian limited nuclear use in a regional conflict is a high U.S. and NATO priority."*

16   *On November 16, 2021, following a virtual meeting the previous day between China's President*

Xi Jinping and President Biden, White House national security advisor Jake Sullivan stated that "the two leaders agreed that we would look to begin to carry forward discussions on strategic stability," and that "it is now incumbent on us to think about the most productive way to carry it forward from here."47 A November 17, 2021, press report stated The United States and China will aim to have 'conversations' on arms control, 'not formal talks', the White House National Security Council said on Wednesday [November 17], downplaying contact on the issue following a meeting between the two countries' leaders

17   *"If that's the argument that Beijing is giving, we're not asking to have a discussion about numbers. We're saying, let's talk about putting some guardrails into the relationship so that we don't have unnecessary crises," he said. Johnson added that if Beijing preferred to not engage bilaterally, it could "demonstrate some transparency" about its nuclear build-up through the International Atomic Energy Agency by declaring its plutonium stocks for civilian purposes. "The Chinese have stopped doing that, and that's a real concern," he said.*

18   *The benefits, costs, and risks of forward-deploying U.S. forces to distant regions on a sustained basis rather than basing them in the United States and deploying them to distant regions in response to specific contingencies is a long-standing issue in U.S. defense planning. Regarding the regional distribution of U.S. military capabilities and force deployments, U.S. officials since at least 2006 have expressed desires (or announced plans) for bolstering U.S. military capabilities and force deployments in the Indo-Pacific region so as to counter China's growing military capabilities. On the other hand, Russia's actions in Europe and developments in the Middle East pose their own security challenges, and some observers express concern about a scenario in which the United States could*

20   *On February 4, 2021, President Biden announced that "Defense Secretary Austin will be leading a Global Posture Review of our forces so that our military footprint is appropriately aligned with our foreign policy and national security priorities."*

22   *"As mentioned above, Russia's invasion of multiple parts of Ukraine starting on February 24, 2022, has prompted increased discussion of how much priority U.S. defense planning should give to Europe (to deter and respond to Russian actions) versus the Indo-Pacific (to deter China), how the U.S. response to Russia's actions in Ukraine might influence China's calculations regarding potential actions it might take toward Taiwan, and whether the tension about how to address concerns about both China and Russia should lead to changes in U.S. grand strategy or defense strategy, and/or the size of the U.S. defense budget."*

23   *"The emergence of GPC with China has led to a major U.S. defense-planning focus on strengthening U.S. military capabilities in the Indo-Pacific region. U.S. officials since 2006 have expressed desires (or announced plans) for bolstering U.S. military capabilities and force deployments in the Indo-Pacific region for the purpose of countering China's growing military capabilities."*

24   *"The Department will support Taiwan's asymmetric self-defense commensurate with the evolving PRC threat and consistent with our one China policy. We will work with the ROK to continue to improve its defense capability to lead the Alliance combined defense, with U.S. forces augmenting those of the ROK. We will invigorate multilateral approaches to security challenges in the region, to include by promoting the role of the Association of Southeast Asian Nations in addressing regional security issues. The*

Department will work with Allies and partners to ensure power projection in a contested environment. The Department will also support Ally and partner efforts, in accordance with U.S. policy and international law, to address acute forms of gray zone coercion from the PRC's campaigns to establish control over

25 Regarding the origin of the PDI, in April 2020, it was reported that Admiral Philip (Phil) Davidson, Commander of U.S. Indo-Pacific Command (INDOPACOM), had submitted to Congress a $20.1 billion plan for investments for improving U.S. military capabilities in the Indo-Pacific region. Davidson submitted the plan, entitled Regain the Advantage, in response to Section 1253 of the FY2020 National Defense Authorization Act (S. 1790/P.L. 116-92 of December 20, 2019), which required the Commander of INDOPACOM to submit to the congressional defense committees a report providing the Commander's independent assessment of the activities and resources required, for FY2022-F

26 The Biden Administration's October 2022 NDS states Europe. The Department will maintain its bedrock commitment to NATO collective security, working alongside Allies and partners to deter, defend, and build resilience against further Russian military aggression and acute forms of gray zone coercion. As we continue contributing to NATO capabilities and readiness—including through improvements to our posture in Europe and our extended nuclear deterrence commitments—the Department will work with Allies bilaterally and through NATO's established processes to better focus NATO capability development and military modernization to address Russia's military threat. The approach will emphasize ready, interoperable combat power in contested environments across NATO forces, particularly air forces and other joint precision strike capabilities, and critical enablers such as intelligence, surveillance, and reconnaissance (ISR

27 The emergence of GPC has led to a focus by U.S. military services on the development of new operational concepts—that is, new ways of employing U.S. military forces—particularly for countering improving Chinese anti-access/area-denial (A2/AD) forces in the Indo-Pacific region. These new operational concepts include Multi-Domain Operations (MDO) for the Army and Air Force, Agile Combat Employment for the Air Force, Distributed Maritime Operations (DMO) for the Navy and Marine Corps, and Expeditionary Advanced Base Operations (EABO) for the Marine Corps. In general, these new operational concepts are more distributed and networked, make greater use of unmanned vehicles, and employ a higher degree of integration between operating domains

29 As part of the renewed emphasis on capabilities for high-end conventional warfare, DOD officials have expressed concern that U.S. superiority in conventional weapon technologies has narrowed or in some cases been eliminated by China and (in certain areas) Russia. In response, DOD has taken a number of actions that are intended to help maintain or regain U.S. superiority in conventional weapon technologies, including increased research and development funding for new militarily applicable technologies such as artificial intelligence (AI), autonomous unmanned weapons, hypersonic weapons, directed-energy weapons, biotechnology, and quantum technology.

30 "Successful competition requires imagining our military capability as an ever-evolving collective, not a static inventory of weapons in development or sustainment. In many cases, effective competition benefits from sidestepping symmetric arms races and instead comes from the creative application of new concepts with emerging science and technology."

31 "Our current system is too slow and too focused on acquiring systems not designed to address the most critical challenges we now face. This orientation leaves little incentive

to design open systems that can rapidly incorporate cutting-edge technologies, creating longer-term challenges with obsolescence, interoperability, and cost effectiveness. The Department will instead reward rapid experimentation, acquisition, and fielding. We will better align requirements, resourcing, and acquisition, and undertake a campaign of learning to identify the most promising concepts, incorporating emerging technologies in the commercial and military sectors for solving our key operational challenges."

32   "DOD officials and other observers argue that to facilitate greater innovation and speed in weapon system development and deployment, U.S. defense acquisition policy and the oversight paradigm for assessing the success of acquisition programs will need to be adjusted to place a greater emphasis on innovation and speed as measures of merit in defense acquisition policy, alongside more traditional measures of merit such as minimizing cost growth, schedule delays, and problems in testing. As a consequence, they argue, defense acquisition policy and the oversight paradigm for assessing the success of acquisition programs should place more emphasis on time as a risk factor and feature more experimentation, risk-taking, and tolerance of failure during development, with a lack of failures in testing potentially being viewed in some cases not as an indication of success, but of inadequate

33   Some observers have expressed concern about the adequacy of U.S. mobilization capabilities, particularly since this was not a major defense-planning concern during the 20 to 25 years of the post–Cold War era, and have recommended various actions to improve those capabilities.

34   Concerns over U.S. industrial mobilization capabilities have been reinforced by the U.S. and allied response to Russia's invasion of multiple parts of Ukraine starting on February 24, 2022, which has spotlighted how rapidly certain weapons (particularly precision-guided munitions) can be expended in modern warfare; the finite U.S. and allied inventories of precision-guided munitions, air-defense systems, and other equipment; and limits on existing U.S. and allied industrial capacity for producing new weapons and equipment to replace those transferred to Ukraine and to increase the size of U.S. and allied inventories to levels higher than those that were planned prior to Russia's invasion.

35   "If a war against a major adversary breaks out, it's going to require the military to resupply troops at a pace it hasn't seen in a long time, Air Force Gen. Jacqueline Van Ovost, head of U.S. Transportation Command, said on Wednesday [February 2]. And to keep up with that frenetic tempo, TRANSCOM is going to have to use machine learning and artificial intelligence to streamline its logistics operations, Van Ovost said in an online conversation hosted by the Center for Strategic and International Studies. 'We can't afford to sift through reams and reams of data' in a major war, Van Ovost said. 'We really do need to apply machine learning and artificial intelligence to turn that

36   "The US navy secretary has warned that the 'fragile' American supply chain for military warships means the Pentagon is at risk of having to rely on adversaries such as Russia and China for critical components. Richard Spencer, [who was then] the US navy's top civilian, told the Financial Times he had ordered a review this year that found many contractors were reliant on single suppliers for certain high-tech and high-precision parts, increasing the likelihood they would have to be procured from geostrategic rivals. Mr Spencer said the US was engaged in 'great power competition' with other global rivals and that several of them—'primarily Russia and China'—were 'all of a sudden in your supply chain, [which is] not to the

37   "Russia employs disinformation, cyber, and space operations against the United States and our Allies and partners, and irregular proxy forces in multiple countries. Other state

actors, particularly North Korea and Iran, use similar if currently more limited means. The proliferation of advanced missiles, uncrewed aircraft systems, and cyber tools to military proxies allows competitors to threaten U.S. forces, Allies, and partners, in indirect and deniable ways."

41 "Observers view GPC not as a bipolar situation (like the Cold War) or a unipolar situation (like the post–Cold War era) but as a situation characterized in substantial part by renewed competition among three major world powers—the United States, China, and Russia."

42 "In February 2007, in a speech at an international security conference in Munich, Russian President Vladimir Putin criticized and rejected the concept of a unipolar power, predicted a shift to multipolar order, and affirmed an active Russian role in international affairs. Some observers view the speech in retrospect as prefiguring a more assertive and competitive Russian foreign policy."

43 "Some observers are describing the current situation of GPC as a new Cold War (or Cold War II or 2.0), particularly since Russia's invasion of multiple parts of Ukraine starting on February 24, 2022. That term may have utility in referring specifically to current U.S.-Russian or U.S.-Chinese relations. The original Cold War, however, was a bipolar situation with the United States and Russia, while the current situation of GPC is a three-power situation involving the United States, China, and Russia. The bipolarity of the Cold War, moreover, was reinforced by the opposing NATO and Warsaw Pact alliances, whereas in contrast, neither Russia nor China today lead an equivalent of the Warsaw Pact. And while terrorists were a

44 "Observers viewing the current situation have given it various names, but names using some variation of great power competition or renewed great power competition appear to have become the most commonly used in public policy discussions."

86 "In general, the BUR reshaped the U.S. military into a force that was smaller than the Cold War U.S. military, and oriented toward a planning scenario being able to conduct two major regional contingencies (MRCs) rather than the Cold War planning scenario of a NATO-Warsaw Pact conflict."

THE SPACE POWER SERIES AND SPACE SENTINEL

This publication is part of the Space Power series from Nimble Books, which offers a wide selection of both copyrighted and public domain works on space power and space warfare. The Space Power series is integrated with the Nimble Books AI service, Space Sentinel.

Space Sentinel is a specialized version of ChatGPT focused on the realms of space and national security. Its purpose is to provide authoritative and precise information in these fields. Its approach is grounded in professionalism, accuracy, and a deep understanding of space power and security, supported by a suite of tools: DALL-E for visualizations, a browser for research, and Python for analytical tasks. It accesses an extensive specialized knowledge base, including this book as well as other key texts on space doctrine, the space industrial base, and space power, to illuminate the complexities of space with factual depth and clarity. Its role is to guide and inform.

Available via the GPT Store at OpenAI. Currently limited to users of ChatGPT Plus.

https://chat.openai.com/g/g-JmYFkkrr7-space-sentinel

Great Power Competition: Implications for Defense—Issues for Congress

Updated October 3, 2023

Congressional Research Service

https://crsreports.congress.gov

R43838

Summary

The emergence over the past decade of intensified U.S. competition with the People's Republic of China (PRC or China) and the Russian Federation (Russia)—often referred to as great power competition (GPC) or strategic competition—has profoundly changed the conversation about U.S. defense issues from what it was during the post–Cold War era: Counterterrorist operations and U.S. military operations in the Middle East—which had been more at the center of discussions of U.S. defense issues following the terrorist attacks of September 11, 2001—are now a less-prominent element in the conversation, and the conversation now focuses more on the following elements, all of which relate largely to China and/or Russia:

- grand strategy and geopolitics as a starting point for discussing U.S. defense issues;
- the force-planning standard, meaning the number and types of simultaneous or overlapping conflicts or other contingencies that the U.S. military should be sized to be able to conduct—a planning factor that can strongly impact the size of the U.S. defense budget;
- organizational changes within the Department of Defense (DOD);
- nuclear weapons, nuclear deterrence, and nuclear arms control;
- global U.S. military posture;
- U.S. and allied military capabilities in the Indo-Pacific region;
- U.S. and NATO military capabilities in Europe;
- new U.S. military service operational concepts;
- capabilities for conducting so-called high-end conventional warfare;
- maintaining U.S. superiority in conventional weapon technologies;
- innovation and speed of U.S. weapon system development and deployment;
- mobilization capabilities for an extended-length large-scale conflict;
- supply chain security, meaning awareness and minimization of reliance in U.S. military systems on foreign components, subcomponents, materials, and software; and
- capabilities for countering so-called hybrid warfare and gray-zone tactics.

The issue for Congress is how U.S. defense planning and budgeting should respond to GPC and whether to approve, reject, or modify the Biden Administration's defense strategy and proposed funding levels, plans, and programs for addressing GPC. Congress's decisions on these issues could have significant implications for U.S. defense capabilities and funding requirements and the U.S. defense industrial base.

Contents

Introduction 1

Background 1

   Great Power Competition.. 1

      Overview.. 1

      Obama Administration and Trump Administration Strategy Documents 2

      Biden Administration October 2022 National Security Strategy....................................... 2

      Biden Administration October 2022 National Defense Strategy 4

   Overview of Implications for Defense.. 6

      Grand Strategy and Geopolitics 6

      Force-Planning Standard.. 8

      Organizational Changes within DOD 9

      Nuclear Weapons, Nuclear Deterrence, and Nuclear Arms Control 10

      Global U.S. Military Posture 15

      U.S. and Allied Capabilities in Indo-Pacific Region 21

      U.S. and NATO Capabilities in Europe 24

      New Operational Concepts 25

      Capabilities for High-End Conventional Warfare.. 25

      Maintaining U.S. Superiority in Conventional Weapon Technologies 27

      Innovation and Speed of U.S. Weapon System Development and Deployment............... 29

      Mobilization Capabilities for Extended-Length Conflict 31

      Supply Chain Security 33

      Capabilities for Countering Hybrid Warfare and Gray-Zone Tactics 34

Issues for Congress.. 35

Appendixes

Appendix A. Transition from Post–Cold War Era to GPC 38

Appendix B. Articles on Transition to GPC and GPC in General.. 43

Appendix C. Articles on Grand Strategy and Geopolitics.. 53

Appendix D. Readings on Supply Chain Security 69

Appendix E. Articles on Russian and Chinese Irregular, Hybrid, and Gray-Zone Warfare 75

Appendix F. Congress and the Late 1980s/Early 1990s Transition to Post–Cold War Era 84

Contacts

Author Information.. 86

Introduction

This report provides a brief overview of some implications for U.S. defense of intensified U.S. competition with the People's Republic of China (PRC or China) and the Russian Federation (Russia), often referred to as great power competition (GPC) or strategic competition. The issue for Congress is how U.S. defense planning and budgeting should respond to GPC, and whether to approve, reject, or modify the Biden Administration's defense strategy and proposed funding levels, plans, and programs for addressing GPC. Congress's decisions on these issues could have significant implications for U.S. defense capabilities and funding requirements and the U.S. defense industrial base.

This report focuses on defense-related issues and does not discuss potential implications of GPC for other policy areas, such as foreign policy and diplomacy, trade and finance, energy, and foreign assistance.

Background

Great Power Competition

Overview

The post–Cold War era of international relations—which began in the early 1990s[1] and is generally characterized as having featured reduced levels of overt political, ideological, and military competition among major states—showed initial signs of fading in 2006-2008 and by 2014 had given way to a situation of intensified U.S. competition with China as well as Russia, as well as challenges by China and Russia to elements of the U.S.-led international order established after World War II.[2] For some observers, the ending of the post–Cold War era and emergence of GPC has been underscored by China and Russia's announced strategic partnership and by Russia's invasion of multiple parts of Ukraine starting on February 24, 2022.[3]

---

[1] As the term suggests, the post–Cold war era emerged following the end of the Cold War between the United States and the Soviet Union. As discussed in **Appendix A**, key events marking the end of the Cold War include the fall of the Berlin Wall in November 1989, the disbanding of the Soviet-led Warsaw Pact military alliance in March 1991, and the dissolution of the Soviet Union into Russia and the former Soviet republics in December 1991. The post–Cold War era is sometimes referred to as the unipolar moment, with the United States as the unipolar power.

[2] For further discussion of the transition from the post–Cold War era of international relations to the current situation of great power competition, including initial signs of the fading of the post–Cold War era in 2006-2008, see **Appendix A**. The term *international order* is generally used to refer to the collection of organizations, institutions, treaties, rules, and norms that are intended to organize, structure, and regulate international relations during a given historical period. Key features of the U.S.-led international order established at the end of World War II—also known as the liberal international order, postwar international order, or open international order, and often referred to as a rules-based order—are generally said to include the following: respect for the territorial integrity of countries, and the unacceptability of changing international borders by force or coercion; a preference for resolving disputes between countries peacefully, without the use or threat of use of force or coercion; strong international institutions; respect for international law and human rights; a preference for free markets and free trade; and the treatment of international waters, international air space, outer space, and (more recently) cyberspace as international commons. For additional discussion of the term *international order*, see CRS Report R44891, *U.S. Role in the World: Background and Issues for Congress*, by Ronald O'Rourke and Michael Moodie.

[3] See, for example, some of the articles dated from late February 2022 into March 2022 that are listed in **Appendix B**. Some observers, in discussing China and Russia's announced strategic partnership, use terms other than *partnership*, such as *alignment*, *convergence*, *coordination*, or *alliance*. For more China and Russia's announced strategic
(continued...)

For additional background information and a list of articles on the transition from the post–Cold War era to GPC, see **Appendix A** and **Appendix B**.

Obama Administration and Trump Administration Strategy Documents

The emergence of GPC was acknowledged alongside other considerations in the Obama Administration's June 2015 National Military Strategy.[4] It was placed at the center of the Trump Administration's December 2017 National Security Strategy[5] and January 2018 National Defense Strategy,[6] which formally reoriented U.S. national security strategy and U.S. defense strategy toward an explicit primary focus on GPC.

Biden Administration October 2022 National Security Strategy

The Biden Administration's October 2022 National Security Strategy (NSS) states

> We face two strategic challenges. The first is that the post-Cold War era is definitively over and a competition is underway between the major powers to shape what comes next....
>
> The second is that while this competition is underway, people all over the world are struggling to cope with the effects of shared challenges that cross borders—whether it is climate change, food insecurity, communicable diseases, terrorism, energy shortages, or inflation.[7]

Regarding competition with China and Russia and challenges to the international order, the October 2022 NSS's first part, entitled "The Competition for What Comes Next," includes the following statements, among others:

- "The basic laws and principles governing relations among nations, including the United Nations Charter and the protection it affords all states from being invaded by their neighbors or having their borders redrawn by force, are under attack. The risk of conflict between major powers is increasing" (p. 7).

- "The most pressing strategic challenge facing our vision is from powers that layer authoritarian governance with a revisionist foreign policy. It is their behavior that poses a challenge to international peace and stability—especially waging or preparing for wars of aggression, actively undermining the democratic political processes of other countries, leveraging technology and supply chains for coercion and repression, and exporting an illiberal model of international order. Many non-democracies join the world's democracies in forswearing these behaviors. Unfortunately, Russia and the People's Republic of China (PRC) do not" (p. 8).

---

partnership, see CRS In Focus IF12100, *China-Russia Relations*, by Ricardo Barrios and Andrew S. Bowen; and CRS In Focus IF12120, *China's Economic and Trade Ties with Russia*, by Karen M. Sutter and Michael D. Sutherland. See also CRS In Focus IF11885, *De-Dollarization Efforts in China and Russia*, by Rebecca M. Nelson and Karen M. Sutter; and CRS In Focus IF11514, *Power of Siberia: A Natural Gas Pipeline Brings Russia and China Closer*, by Michael Ratner and Heather L. Greenley.

[4] Department of Defense, *The National Military Strategy of the United States of America 2015, The United States Military's Contribution To National Security*, June 2015, pp. i, 1-4.

[5] Office of the President, *National Security Strategy of the United States of America*, December 2017, 55 pp.

[6] Department of Defense, *Summary of the 2018 National Defense Strategy of the United States of America: Sharpening the American Military's Competitive Edge*, undated but released January 2018, 11 pp.

[7] White House, *National Security Strategy*, October 2022, p. 6.

- "Russia and the PRC pose different challenges. Russia poses an immediate threat to the free and open international system, recklessly flouting the basic laws of the international order today, as its brutal war of aggression against Ukraine has shown. The PRC, by contrast, is the only competitor with both the intent to reshape the international order and, increasingly, the economic, diplomatic, military, and technological power to advance that objective" (p. 8).

- "In their own ways, [China and Russia] now seek to remake the international order to create a world conducive to their highly personalized and repressive type of autocracy" (pp. 8-9).

- The United States will, among other things, "modernize and strengthen [its] military so it is equipped for the era of strategic competition with major powers, while maintaining the capability to disrupt the terrorist threat to the homeland" (p. 11).

- "[T]his strategy recognizes that the PRC presents America's most consequential geopolitical challenge.... Russia poses an immediate and ongoing threat to the regional security order in Europe and it is a source of disruption and instability globally but it lacks the across the spectrum capabilities of the PRC" (p. 8).

- "This decade will be decisive, in setting the terms of our competition with the PRC, managing the acute threat posed by Russia, and in our efforts to deal with shared challenges, particularly climate change, pandemics, and economic turbulence" (pp. 12-13).

The October 2022 NSS's third part, entitled "Our Global Priorities," includes a section entitled "Out-Competing China and Constraining Russia" that includes the following statements, among others:

- "The PRC and Russia are increasingly aligned with each other but the challenges they pose are, in important ways, distinct. We will prioritize maintaining an enduring competitive edge over the PRC while constraining a still profoundly dangerous Russia" (p. 23).

- "The PRC is the only competitor with both the intent to reshape the international order and, increasingly, the economic, diplomatic, military, and technological power to do it. Beijing has ambitions to create an enhanced sphere of influence in the Indo-Pacific and to become the world's leading power. It is using its technological capacity and increasing influence over international institutions to create more permissive conditions for its own authoritarian model, and to mold global technology use and norms to privilege its interests and values" (p. 23).

- "Over the past decade, the Russian government has chosen to pursue an imperialist foreign policy with the goal of overturning key elements of the international order. This culminated in a full-scale invasion of Ukraine in an attempt to topple its government and bring it under Russian control. But, this attack did not come out of the blue; it was preceded by Russia's 2014 invasion of Ukraine, its military intervention in Syria, its longstanding efforts to destabilize its neighbors using intelligence and cyber capabilities, and its blatant attempts to undermine internal democratic processes in countries across Europe, Central Asia, and around the world" (p. 25).

The NSS's second part, entitled "Investing in Our Strength," includes a section entitled "Modernizing and Strengthening Our Military" that includes the following statements, among others:

- "The military will act urgently to sustain and strengthen deterrence, with the PRC as its pacing challenge " (p. 20).

- "The United States has a vital interest in deterring aggression by the PRC, Russia, and other states. More capable competitors and new strategies of threatening behavior below and above the traditional threshold of conflict mean we cannot afford to rely solely on conventional forces and nuclear deterrence. Our defense strategy must sustain and strengthen deterrence, with the PRC as our pacing challenge. Our National Defense Strategy relies on integrated deterrence: the seamless combination of capabilities to convince potential adversaries that the costs of their hostile activities outweigh their benefits" (p. 22).

Biden Administration October 2022 National Defense Strategy

The Biden Administration's October 2022 National Defense Strategy (NDS) states that it "directs the Department [of Defense] to act urgently to sustain and strengthen U.S. deterrence, with the People's Republic of China (PRC) as the Department's pacing challenge." The document states further that it

> advances a strategy focused on the PRC and on collaboration with our growing network of Allies and partners on common objectives. It seeks to prevent the PRC's dominance of key regions while protecting the U.S. homeland and reinforcing a stable and open international system. Consistent with the 2022 National Security Strategy (NSS), a key objective of the NDS is to dissuade the PRC from considering aggression as a viable means of advancing goals that threaten vital U.S. national interests. Conflict with the PRC is neither inevitable nor desirable. The Department's priorities support broader whole-of-government efforts to develop terms of interaction with the PRC that are favorable to our interests and values, while managing strategic competition and enabling the pursuit of cooperation on common challenges.
>
> Even as we focus on the PRC as our pacing challenge, the NDS also accounts for the acute threat posed by Russia, demonstrated most recently by Russia's unprovoked further invasion of Ukraine. The Department will support robust deterrence of Russian aggression against vital U.S. national interests, including our treaty Allies. We will work closely with the North Atlantic Treaty Organization (NATO) and our partners to provide U.S. leadership, develop key enabling capabilities, and deepen interoperability. In service of our strategic priorities, we will accept measured risk but remain vigilant in the face of other persistent threats, including those posed by North Korea, Iran, and violent extremist organizations (VEOs). We will also build resilience in the face of destabilizing and potentially catastrophic transboundary challenges such as climate change and pandemics, which increasingly strain the Joint Force [i.e., U.S. military].[8]

Regarding China, the October 2022 NDS states

> The most comprehensive and serious challenge to U.S. national security is the PRC's coercive and increasingly aggressive endeavor to refashion the Indo-Pacific region and the international system to suit its interests and authoritarian preferences. The PRC seeks to undermine U.S. alliances and security partnerships in the Indo-Pacific region, and leverage its growing capabilities, including its economic influence and the People's Liberation Army's (PLA)[9] growing strength and military footprint, to coerce its neighbors and

---

[8] Department of Defense, *2022 National Defense Strategy of the United States of America*, cover letter dated October 27, 2022, p. 2.

[9] China's military as a whole is referred to as the People's Liberation Army (PLA); the term thus refers not only to China's army but to the various military services that constitute China's military. For an overview of the PLA, see CRS (continued...)

threaten their interests. The PRC's increasingly provocative rhetoric and coercive activity towards Taiwan are destabilizing, risk miscalculation, and threaten the peace and stability of the Taiwan Strait. This is part of a broader pattern of destabilizing and coercive PRC behavior that stretches across the East China Sea, the South China Sea, and along the Line of Actual Control [between China and India]. The PRC has expanded and modernized nearly every aspect of the PLA, with a focus on offsetting U.S. military advantages. The PRC is therefore the pacing challenge for the Department.

In addition to expanding its conventional forces, the PLA is rapidly advancing and integrating its space, counterspace, cyber, electronic, and informational warfare capabilities to support its holistic approach to joint warfare. The PLA seeks to target the ability of the Joint Force [i.e., U.S. military] to project power to defend vital U.S. interests and aid our Allies in a crisis or conflict. The PRC is also expanding the PLA's global footprint and working to establish a more robust overseas and basing infrastructure to allow it to project military power at greater distances. In parallel, the PRC is accelerating the modernization and expansion of its nuclear capabilities. The United States and its Allies and partners will increasingly face the challenge of deterring two major powers with modern and diverse nuclear capabilities—the PRC and Russia—creating new stresses on strategic stability.[10]

The October 2022 NDS also states

Deterring PRC Attacks. The Department will bolster deterrence by leveraging existing and emergent force capabilities, posture, and activities to enhance denial, and by enhancing the resilience of U.S. systems the PRC may seek to target. We will develop new operational concepts and enhanced future warfighting capabilities against potential PRC aggression. Collaboration with Allies and partners will cement joint capability with the aid of multilateral exercises, codevelopment of technologies, greater intelligence and information sharing, and combined planning for shared deterrence challenges. We will also build enduring advantages, undertaking foundational improvements and enhancements to ensure our technological edge and Joint Force [i.e., U.S. military] combat credibility.[11]

Regarding Russia, the October 2022 NDS states

Even as the PRC poses the Department's pacing challenge, recent events underscore the acute threat posed by Russia. Contemptuous of its neighbors' independence, Russia's government seeks to use force to impose border changes and to reimpose an imperial sphere of influence. Its extensive track record of territorial aggression includes the escalation of its brutal, unprovoked war against Ukraine. Although its leaders' political and military actions intended to fracture NATO have backfired dramatically, the goal remains. Russia presents serious, continuing risks in key areas. These include nuclear threats to the homeland and U.S. Allies and partners; long-range cruise missile threats; cyber and information operations; counterspace threats; chemical and biological weapons (CBW); undersea warfare; and extensive gray zone campaigns targeted against democracies in particular. Russia has incorporated these capabilities and methods into an overall strategy that, like the PRC's, seeks to exploit advantages in geography and time backed by a mix of threats to the U.S. homeland and to our Allies and partners.[12]

In Focus IF11719, *China Primer: The People's Liberation Army (PLA)*, by Caitlin Campbell, and CRS Report R46808, *China's Military: The People's Liberation Army (PLA)*, by Caitlin Campbell.

[10] Department of Defense, *2022 National Defense Strategy of the United States of America*, cover letter dated October 27, 2022, p. 4.

[11] Department of Defense, *2022 National Defense Strategy of the United States of America*, cover letter dated October 27, 2022, p. 10. Italics as in original.

[12] Department of Defense, *2022 National Defense Strategy of the United States of America*, cover letter dated October 27, 2022, p. 5.

The October 2022 NDS also states

> *Deterring Russian Attacks.* The Department will focus on deterring Russian attacks on the United States, NATO members, and other Allies, reinforcing our iron-clad treaty commitments, to include conventional aggression that has the potential to escalate to nuclear employment of any scale. We will work together with our Allies and partners to modernize denial capabilities, increase interoperability, improve resilience against attack and coercion, share intelligence, and strengthen extended nuclear deterrence. Over time, the Department will focus on enhancing denial capabilities and key enablers in NATO's force planning, while NATO Allies seek to bolster their conventional warfighting capabilities. For Ally and partner countries that border Russia, the Department will support efforts to build out response options that enable cost imposition.[13]

The October 2022 NDS states that

> in support of a stable and open international system and our defense commitments, the Department's priorities are:
>
> — Defending the homeland, paced to the growing multi-domain threat posed by the PRC;
>
> — Deterring strategic attacks against the United States, Allies, and partners;
>
> — Deterring aggression, while being prepared to prevail in conflict when necessary—prioritizing the PRC challenge in the Indo-Pacific region, then the Russia challenge in Europe; and,
>
> — Building a resilient Joint Force [i.e., U.S. military] and defense ecosystem.[14]

Overview of Implications for Defense

The emergence of GPC has profoundly changed the conversation about U.S. defense issues from what it was during the post–Cold War era: Counterterrorist operations and U.S. military operations in the Middle East—which had been more at the center of discussions of U.S. defense issues following the terrorist attacks of September 11, 2001—are now a less-prominent element in the conversation, and the conversation now focuses more on the topics discussed briefly in the sections below, all of which relate largely to China and/or Russia.[15]

Grand Strategy and Geopolitics

The emergence of GPC has led to a renewed emphasis on grand strategy and geopolitics[16] as a starting point for discussing U.S. defense funding levels, strategy, plans, and programs. A November 2, 2015, press report, for example, stated the following:

---

[13] Department of Defense, *2022 National Defense Strategy of the United States of America*, cover letter dated October 27, 2022, p. 10. Italics as in original.

[14] Department of Defense, *2022 National Defense Strategy of the United States of America*, cover letter dated October 27, 2022, p. 7. The document defines the defense ecosystem on page 2 as "the Department of Defense, the defense industrial base, and the array of private sector and academic enterprises that create and sharpen the Joint Force's [i.e., U.S. military's] technological edge."

[15] For a press report that provides an overview discussion of this shift in the conversation, see Michael R. Gordon, "The U.S. Is Not Yet Ready For 'Great Power' Conflict," *Wall Street Journal*, March 6, 2023.

[16] The term *grand strategy* generally refers to a country's overall strategy for securing its interests and making its way in the world, using all the national tools at its disposal, including diplomatic, information, military, and economic tools (sometimes abbreviated in U.S. government parlance as DIME).

The term *geopolitics* is often used as a synonym for international politics or strategy relating to international politics. (continued...)

> The resurgence of Russia and the continued rise of China have created a new period of great-power rivalry—and a corresponding need for a solid grand strategy, [then-]U.S. Deputy Defense Secretary Robert Work said Monday at the Defense One Summit in Washington, DC.
>
> "The era of everything [i.e., multiple international security challenges] is the era of grand strategy," Work said, suggesting that the United States must carefully marshal and deploy its great yet limited resources.[17]

For the United States, grand strategy can be viewed as strategy at a global or interregional level, as opposed to U.S. strategies for individual regions, countries, or issues. From a U.S. perspective on grand strategy and geopolitics, it can be noted that most of the world's people, resources, and economic activity are located not in the Western Hemisphere, but in the other hemisphere, particularly Eurasia. In response to this basic feature of world geography, U.S. policymakers for the last several decades have chosen to pursue, as a key element of U.S. national strategy, a goal of preventing the emergence of regional hegemons in Eurasia. Although U.S. policymakers do not often state explicitly in public the goal of preventing the emergence of regional hegemons in Eurasia, U.S. military operations in recent decades—both wartime operations and day-to-day operations—appear to have been carried out in no small part in support of this goal.

The goal of preventing the emergence of regional hegemons in Eurasia is a major reason why the U.S. military is structured with force elements that enable it to deploy from the United States, cross broad expanses of ocean and air space, and then conduct sustained, large-scale military operations upon arrival in Eurasia or the waters and airspace surrounding Eurasia. Force elements associated with this goal include, among other things, an Air Force with significant numbers of long-range bombers, long-range surveillance aircraft, long-range airlift aircraft, and aerial refueling tankers, and a Navy with significant numbers of aircraft carriers, nuclear-powered attack submarines, large surface combatants, large amphibious ships, and underway replenishment ships.[18]

The U.S. goal of preventing the emergence of regional hegemons in Eurasia, though long-standing, is not written in stone—it is a policy choice reflecting two judgments: (1) that given the amount of people, resources, and economic activity in Eurasia, a regional hegemon in Eurasia would represent a concentration of power large enough to be able to threaten vital U.S. interests; and (2) that Eurasia is not dependably self-regulating in terms of preventing the emergence of regional hegemons, meaning that the countries of Eurasia cannot be counted on to be able to prevent, though their own actions, the emergence of regional hegemons, and may need assistance from one or more countries outside Eurasia to be able to do this dependably.

An emergence of GPC does not require an acceptance of both of these judgments as guideposts for U.S. defense in coming years—one might accept that there has been an emergence of GPC but nevertheless conclude that one of these judgments or the other, while perhaps valid in the past, is no longer valid. A conclusion that one of these judgments is not valid could lead to a potentially

---

More specifically, it refers to the influence of basic geographic features on international relations, and to the analysis of international relations from a perspective that places a strong emphasis on the influence of such geographic features. Basic geographic features involved in geopolitical analysis include things such as the relative sizes and locations of countries or land masses; the locations of key resources such as oil or water; geographic barriers such as oceans, deserts, and mountain ranges; and key transportation links such as roads, railways, and waterways. For further discussion, see Daniel H. Deudney, "Geopolitics," *Encyclopedia Britannica*, June 12, 2013, accessed November 17, 2021, at https://www.britannica.com/topic/geopolitics.

[17] Bradley Peniston, "Work: 'The Age of Everything Is the Era of Grand Strategy'," *Defense One*, November 2, 2015.

[18] For additional discussion, see CRS In Focus IF10485, *Defense Primer: Geography, Strategy, and U.S. Force Design*, by Ronald O'Rourke.

major change in U.S. grand strategy that could lead to large-scale changes in U.S. defense funding levels, strategy, plans, and programs. By the same token, an emergence of GPC does not by itself suggest that these two judgements—and the consequent U.S. goal of preventing the emergence of regional hegemons in Eurasia—are not valid as guideposts for U.S. defense in coming years.

For a list of articles pertaining to the debate over U.S. grand strategy, see **Appendix C**.

Force-Planning Standard

Related to the above issue concerning U.S. grand strategy, the emergence of GPC has prompted renewed discussion of the force-planning standard,[19] meaning the number and types of simultaneous or overlapping conflicts or other contingencies that the U.S. military should be sized to be able to conduct—a planning factor that can strongly impact the size of the U.S. defense budget.

The U.S. military is currently sized to be able to conduct something less than two simultaneous or overlapping major conflicts. At a May 12, 2022, hearing before the Senate Armed Services Committee, for example, Admiral Michael Gilday, the Chief of Naval Operations, was asked what the impact would be on the Navy's ability to meet its operational requirements in Europe if Navy forces were withheld from Europe for the purpose of deterring Chinese aggression in the Pacific. Gilday replied

> I think we'd be challenged. We'd have to take a look at how you squeeze the most out of the joint force [i.e., the overall U.S. military] you have and use it in the best—best possible way. But I think we'd be challenged. You know, right now the force is not sized to handle two simultaneous conflicts. It's—it's sized to fight one and to keep—keep a second adversary in check. But in terms of a two—two all-out conflicts, we are not sized for that.[20]

One observer stated in 2019

> During the post-Cold War era, the U.S. military had a force-planning construct (a scheme that matches the size and capabilities of the force to the key scenarios it is likely to face) focused on fighting two major regional contingencies more or less simultaneously. The idea was that the U.S. should be able to decisively defeat an adversary in the Middle East—Iraq or Iran—without fatally compromising its ability to take on North Korea. This two-war capability was deemed critical to preventing opportunistic aggression by one adversary while the U.S. was engaged with another, and thereby upholding a grand strategy premised on deterring war in multiple regions at once. The two-war strategy, Pentagon officials wrote in 1997, "is the sine qua non of a superpower."

> After the onset of budgetary austerity in 2011, the two-war strategy gradually eroded as defense cuts made it harder to handle two regional adversaries at once. And after the Russian invasion of Ukraine in 2014, it was clear that the U.S. was facing a fundamentally different world, in which the country's foremost adversaries were not inferior rogue states but major powers fielding formidable military capabilities. Add in that any war against Russia or China is likely to occur in their geopolitical backyards, and that both rivals have spent considerable time, money and intellectual effort seeking to neutralize America's ability to project power, and the U.S. military would have enormous difficulty in winning even a single war against a great-power challenger.

---

[19] Other terms for referring to the force-planning standard use *force-sizing* instead of *force-planning*, and *construct* or *metric* instead of *standard*.

[20] Source: CQ transcript of hearing.

In the 2018 National Defense Strategy and subsequent statements, the Pentagon thus outlined a significantly different force-planning construct. It announced that the fully mobilized American military would be capable of *defeating* aggression by a great-power adversary, while also *deterring* (not necessarily defeating) aggression in a second theater. In other words, the U.S. is now building a force not around the demands of two regional conflicts with rogue states, but around the requirements of winning a high-intensity conflict with a single, top-tier competitor—a war with China over Taiwan, for instance, or a clash with Russia in the Baltic region.[21]

The emergence of GPC has prompted some observers to ask whether the force-planning standard should be changed to being able to fight two simultaneous or overlapping major conflicts with adversaries such as China and Russia—a so-called two-war or two-major-war standard.[22] Adopting and implementing a two-war standard relating to potential conflicts with adversaries such as China and Russia could entail substantially expanding the size of the U.S. military and the size of the U.S. defense budget. Whether the United States should adopt or could afford such a two-war force-planning standard is a potentially major issue in U.S. defense planning.

The Biden Administration's October 2022 NDS does not include an explicit statement about the force-planning standard. One observer writing about the October 2022 NDS states

> What is the force sizing construct? The Trump administration said it was one major conflict and "deterring" a second conflict. It is not clear how the demonstration [*sic*: Biden Administration?] is sizing its forces. What size are the services aiming for? Budget documents give some indication … but budget numbers are not necessarily long-term strategic goals. It may be that the classified version of the [2022] NDS, which went to Congress in the spring [of 2022], has answers to all these questions. However, that does not help the public discussion about defense and strategy.[23]

Organizational Changes within DOD

The emergence of GPC has led to increased discussion about whether and how to make organizational changes within the Department of Defense (DOD) to better align DOD's activities with those needed to counter Chinese and, secondarily, Russian military capabilities. Among changes that have been made, among the most prominent have been the creation of the U.S.

---

[21] Hal Brands, "What If the U.S. Could Fight Only One War at a Time?," *Bloomberg*, June 11, 2019. (Also published as Hal Brands, "What If the US Could Fight Only One War at a Time?," American Enterprise Institute, June 11, 2019.) Italics as in original. See also Dakota L. Wood, editor, *2023 Index of U.S. Military Strength*, Heritage Foundation, 2023 (released October 18, 2022), p. 323; Mark Gunzinger and Kamilla Gunzinger, "Ukraine Makes Clear the US Must Reconsider Its One-War Defense Strategy," *Defense News*, March 14, 2022.

[22] See, for example, Eric S. Edelman and Franklin C. Miller, "We Must Return to and Maintain the Two Theater Defense Planning Construct," *Real Clear Defense*, August 17, 2023; Markus Garlauskas, "The United States and Its Allies Must Be Ready to Deter a Two-Front War and Nuclear Attacks in East Asia," Atlantic Council, August 16, 2023; Raphael S. Cohen, "Ukraine and the New Two War Construct," *War on the Rocks*, January 5, 2023; Dakota L. Wood, ed., *2023 Index of U.S. Military Strength*, Heritage Foundation, 2023 (released October 18, 2022), pp. 3, 10, 326, 330, 332; Kori Schake, "America Must Spend More on Defense, How Biden Can Align Resources and Strategy," *Foreign Affairs*, April 5, 2022; Mark Gunzinger and Kamilla Gunzinger, "Ukraine Makes Clear the US Must Reconsider Its One-War Defense Strategy," *Defense News*, March 14, 2022; Hal Brands and Evan Braden Montgomery, "One War Is Not Enough: Strategy and Force Planning for Great-Power Competition," *Texas National Security Review* (Spring 2020), pp. 80-92. See also Hal Brands, "Can the US Take on China, Iran and Russia All at Once?," *Bloomberg*, October 16, 2022.

[23] Mark F. Cancian, "Force Structure in the National Defense Strategy: Highly Capable but Smaller and Less Global," Center for Strategic and International Studies (CSIS), October 31, 2022.

Space Force[24] and the elevation of the U.S. Cyber Command to be its own combatant command.[25] Additional changes are occurring within individual U.S. military services.[26]

Nuclear Weapons, Nuclear Deterrence, and Nuclear Arms Control

The emergence of GPC has led to a renewed emphasis in discussions of U.S. defense on nuclear weapons, nuclear deterrence, and nuclear arms control.[27] Russia's reassertion of its status as a major world power has included, among other things, recurring references by Russian officials to Russia's nuclear weapons capabilities and Russia's status as a major nuclear weapon power.[28] China's nuclear-weapon capabilities are currently much more modest than Russia's, but China reportedly is now modernizing and rapidly increasing its nuclear forces as part of its overall military modernization effort.

The expansion of China's nuclear forces is projected to convert the traditional two-power strategic nuclear deterrent situation between the United States and Russia into a more complex three-power situation. The Biden Administration's October 2022 Nuclear Posture Review (NPR), which was released in conjunction with its October 2022 NDS, states (emphasis as in original):

> By the 2030s the United States will, for the first time in its history, face two major nuclear powers as strategic competitors and potential adversaries. This will create new stresses on stability and new challenges for deterrence, assurance, arms control, and risk reduction....
>
> ***The PRC's nuclear expansion and the changes this could bring to its strategy present new complexities.*** In the near-term, we must factor this into our arms control and risk reduction approaches with Russia. We also recognize that as the security environment evolves, it may be necessary to consider nuclear strategy and force adjustments to assure our ability to achieve deterrence and other objectives for the PRC – even as we continue to

---

[24] See CRS In Focus IF11495, *Defense Primer: The United States Space Force*, coordinated by Kelley M. Sayler.

[25] See CRS In Focus IF10537, *Defense Primer: Cyberspace Operations*, by Catherine A. Theohary.

[26] See, for example, Audrey Decker, "USAF Aims to 'Re-optimize' for Great Power Competition," *Defense One*, September 11, 2023.

[27] See, for example, Hal Brands, "Welcome to the New Era of Nuclear Brinkmanship," *Bloomberg*, August 27, 2023; Francis Gavin, "Time to Rethink America's Nuclear Strategy," *Foreign Affairs*, September 5, 2022; Jeffrey Lewis and Aaron Stein, "Who Is Deterring Whom? The Place of Nuclear Weapons in Modern War," *War on the Rocks*, June 16, 2022; Michael Auslin, "Learning to Think Nuclearly Again, A New Nuclear Era Demands Strategy, Not Just Arms Control," *Foreign Policy*, June 11, 2022; Shlomo Ben-Ami, "Russia's Nuclear Threat Has Worked," *Strategist (ASPI)*, June 8, 2022; Tom Nichols, "We Have No Nuclear Strategy, The U.S. Can't Keep Ignoring the Threat These Weapons Pose," *Atlantic*, June 1, 2022; David E. Sanger and William J. Broad, "Putin's Threats Highlight the Dangers of a New, Riskier Nuclear Era," *New York Times*, June 1, 2022; David Ignatius, "The Pentagon Plans Anew to Head Off an Old Worry: Nuclear War," *Washington Post*, April 28, 2022; Max Hastings, "With Nuclear Threat, Putin Makes the Unthinkable a Possibility, Most Westerners Thought the Peril of Apocalypse Disappeared with the 1991 Collapse of the Soviet Union. They Were Wrong," *Bloomberg*, March 27, 2022; Andreas Kluth, "When, Why and How Putin Might Use Nukes, The Newly Prominent Role of So-Called Tactical Nuclear Weapons Puts the World in the Greatest Danger Since the Cuban Missile Crisis," *Bloomberg*, March 23, 2022; David C. Gompert, "How Putin Exploits America's Fear of Nuclear War," *Wall Street Journal*, March 22, 2022; Patty-Jane Geller, "Putin's Nuclear Threats against Ukraine Demand a NATO Response, Once a Relic of the Cold War, Nuclear Weapons Are Salient Once Again," *Fox News*, March 16, 2022; Sarah Bidgood, "A New Nuclear Arms Race Is a Real Possibility: History Suggests the War in Ukraine Could Put an End to Arms Control As We Know It," *Foreign Policy*, March 15, 2022; Andrew Jeong, "Putin Has Brought Threat of Nuclear Conflict 'Back Within the Realm of Possibility,' U.N. Chief Says," *Washington Post*, March 15, 2022; Patty-Jane Geller, "It's Time to Reconsider Our Nuclear Forces," *Fox News*, March 14, 2022; John D. Maurer, "Maintaining America's Nuclear Deterrent," *War on the Rocks*, March 10, 2022.

[28] See, for example, Dmitry Adamsky, "Russia's New Nuclear Normal, How the Country Has Grown Dangerously Comfortable Brandishing Its Arsenal," *Foreign Affairs*, May 19, 2023.

---

do so for Russia. Our plans and capabilities must also account for the fact that the PRC increasingly will be able to execute a range of nuclear strategies to advance its goals.[29]

Policymakers and deterrence theorists are currently examining how to address this emerging three-power strategic nuclear situation, particularly if it is not bounded and regulated, as the two-power situation was, by a strategic nuclear arms control agreement.[30]

The increased emphasis in discussions of U.S. defense and security on nuclear weapons, nuclear deterrence, and nuclear arms control comes at a time when DOD is in the early stages of a multiyear plan to spend scores of billions of dollars to modernize U.S. strategic nuclear deterrent forces.[31] DOD, for example, currently has plans to acquire a new class of ballistic missile submarines[32] a next-generation long-range bomber,[33] and a next-generation intercontinental ballistic missile.[34]

The October 2022 NSS states

> Nuclear deterrence remains a top priority for the Nation and foundational to integrated deterrence. A safe, secure, and effective nuclear force undergirds our defense priorities by deterring strategic attacks, assuring allies and partners, and allowing us to achieve our objectives if deterrence fails. Our competitors and potential adversaries are investing heavily in new nuclear weapons. By the 2030s, the United States for the first time will need to deter two major nuclear powers, each of whom will field modern and diverse global and regional nuclear forces. To ensure our nuclear deterrent remains responsive to the threats we face, we are modernizing the nuclear Triad, nuclear command, control, and communications, and our nuclear weapons infrastructure, as well as strengthening our extended deterrence commitments to our Allies. We remain equally committed to reducing

---

[29] *2022 Nuclear Posture Review*, pp. 4, 5. The 2022 NPR was released as part of the same document that presents the October 2022 NDS.

[30] See, for example, Robert Peters, *Russia and China Are Running in a Nuclear Arms Race While the United States Is Jogging in Place, Heritage Foundation*, September 13, 2023, 9 pp.; William J. Broad, "The Terror of Threes in the Heavens and on Earth," *New York Times*, June 16 (updated June 30), 2023; Keir Lieber and Daryl G. Press, "US Strategy and Force Posture for an Era of Nuclear Tripolarity," Atlantic Council, May 1, 2023; Brad Roberts, et al., *China's Emergence as a Second Nuclear Peer: Implications for U.S. Nuclear Deterrence Strategy*, Lawrence Livermore National Laboratory, Spring 2023, 74 pp.; David E. Sanger, William J. Broad, and Chris Buckley, "3 Nuclear Superpowers, Rather Than 2, Usher In a New Strategic Era," *New York Times*, April 19, 2023; Greg Torode and Eduardo Baptista, "China's Intensifying Nuclear-Armed Submarine Patrols Add Complexity for U.S., Allies," *Reuters*, April 3, 2023; Jonathan Tirone, "China, Russia Deepen Nuclear Concord That Concerns Pentagon," *Bloomberg*, March 22, 2023; Andrew F. Krepinevich Jr., "The Tripolar Problem," Yale University Press, March 13, 2023; John R. Bolton, "Putin Did the World a Favor by Suspending Russia's Participation in New START," *Washington Post*, March 6, 2023; Greg Torode and Martin Pollard, "Putin's Nuclear Treaty Move Raises Stakes over China's Growing Arsenal," *Reuters*, February 22, 2023; Andrew F. Krepinevich Jr., "How China's Nuclear Ambitions Will Change Deterrence Shifting from a Bipolar System to a Tripolar one," Hudson Institute, January 31, 2023; Robert S. Litwak, *Tripolar Instability, Nuclear Competition Among the United States, Russia, and China*, Wilson Center, 2023 124 pp; Matthew Kroenig, "Arms Racing Under Nuclear Tripolarity: Evidence for an Action-Reaction Cycle?" Atlantic Council, December 20, 2022; Editorial Board, "The Nuclear Arms Race Grows from Two to Three Major Competing Powers," *Washington Post*, November 11, 2022; Katherine Walla, "Inside the US Nuclear Posture Review's Approach to a New Era of Three-Power Nuclear Competition," *Washington Post*, November 3, 2022; Tara Copp, "US Military 'Furiously' Rewriting Nuclear Deterrence to Address Russia and China, STRATCOM Chief Says," *Defense One*, August 11, 2022; Andrew F. Krepinevich Jr., "The New Nuclear Age How China's Growing Nuclear Arsenal Threatens Deterrence," *Foreign Affairs*, May/June 2022 (published April 19, 2022).

[31] See CRS Report RL33640, *U.S. Strategic Nuclear Forces: Background, Developments, and Issues*, by Amy F. Woolf, and Congressional Budget Office, *Projected Costs of U.S. Nuclear Forces, 2021 to 2030*, May 2021, 12 pp.

[32] CRS Report R41129, *Navy Columbia (SSBN-826) Class Ballistic Missile Submarine Program: Background and Issues for Congress*, by Ronald O'Rourke.

[33] See CRS Report R44463, *Air Force B-21 Raider Long-Range Strike Bomber*, coordinated by John R. Hoehn.

[34] See, for example, "Sentinel ICBM," Air Force Nuclear Weapons Center, undated, accessed November 4, 2022.

---

the risks of nuclear war. This includes taking further steps to reduce the role of nuclear weapons in our strategy and pursuing realistic goals for mutual, verifiable arms control, which contribute to our deterrence strategy and strengthen the global non-proliferation regime.[35]

The October 2022 NPR states

In large part due to the actions of our strategic competitors, the international security environment has deteriorated in recent years. The People's Republic of China (PRC) is the overall pacing challenge for U.S. defense planning and a growing factor in evaluating our nuclear deterrent. The PRC has embarked on an ambitious expansion, modernization, and diversification of its nuclear forces and established a nascent nuclear triad. The PRC likely intends to possess at least 1,000 deliverable warheads by the end of the decade.

While the end state resulting from the PRC's specific choices with respect to its nuclear forces and strategy is uncertain, the trajectory of these efforts points to a large, diverse nuclear arsenal with a high degree of survivability, reliability, and effectiveness. This could provide the PRC with new options before and during a crisis or conflict to leverage nuclear weapons for coercive purposes, including military provocations against U.S. Allies and partners in the region.

Russia continues to emphasize nuclear weapons in its strategy, modernize and expand its nuclear forces, and brandish its nuclear weapons in support of its revisionist security policy. Its modern nuclear arsenal, which is expected to grow further, presents an enduring existential threat to the United States and our Allies and partners. For more than twenty years, Russia has pursued a wide-ranging military modernization program that includes replacing legacy strategic nuclear systems and steadily expanding and diversifying nuclear systems that pose a direct threat to NATO and neighboring countries.... Similarly, Russia is pursuing several novel nuclear-capable systems designed to hold the U.S. homeland or Allies and partners at risk, some of which are also not accountable under New START.

By the 2030s the United States will, for the first time in its history, face two major nuclear powers as strategic competitors and potential adversaries. This will create new stresses on stability and new challenges for deterrence, assurance, arms control, and risk reduction.[36]

The October 2022 NPR also states

Russia's invasion of Ukraine underscores that nuclear dangers persist, and could grow, in an increasingly competitive and volatile geopolitical landscape. The Russian Federation's unprovoked and unlawful invasion of Ukraine in 2022 is a stark reminder of nuclear risk in contemporary conflict. Russia has conducted its aggression against Ukraine under a nuclear shadow characterized by irresponsible saber-rattling, out of cycle nuclear exercises, and false narratives concerning the potential use of weapons of mass destruction (WMD). In brandishing Russia's nuclear arsenal in an attempt to intimidate Ukraine and the North Atlantic Treaty Organization (NATO), Russia's leaders have made clear that they view these weapons as a shield behind which to wage unjustified aggression against their neighbors. Irresponsible Russian statements and actions raise the risk of deliberate or unintended escalation. Russia's leadership should have no doubt regarding the resolve of the United States to both resist nuclear coercion and act as a responsible nuclear power.[37]

The October 2022 NPR further states

---

[35] White House, *National Security Strategy*, October 2022, p. 21.

[36] *2022 Nuclear Posture Review*, p. 4. The October 2022 NPR was released as part of the same document that presents the October 2022 NDS.

[37] *2022 Nuclear Posture Review*, pp. 1-2.

The current and growing salience of nuclear weapons in the strategies and forces of our competitors heightens the risks associated with strategic competition and the stakes of crisis and military confrontation. As the NDS notes, we must be able to deter conventional aggression that has the potential to escalate to nuclear employment of any scale. Russia presents the most acute example of this problem today given its significantly larger stockpile of regional nuclear systems and the possibility it would use these forces to try to win a war on its periphery or avoid defeat if it was in danger of losing a conventional war. Deterring Russian limited nuclear use in a regional conflict is a high U.S. and NATO priority.

The PRC's nuclear expansion and the changes this could bring to its strategy present new complexities. In the near-term, we must factor this into our arms control and risk reduction approaches with Russia. We also recognize that as the security environment evolves, it may be necessary to consider nuclear strategy and force adjustments to assure our ability to achieve deterrence and other objectives for the PRC—even as we continue to do so for Russia. Our plans and capabilities must also account for the fact that the PRC increasingly will be able to execute a range of nuclear strategies to advance its goals.[38]

A current question regarding U.S. nuclear force modernization is whether to develop and procure a new nuclear-armed sea-launched cruise missile (SLCM-N) for placement on U.S. Navy attack submarines.[39] The Biden Administration's proposed FY2023 defense budget and its October 2022 NPR proposed canceling the SLCM-N program.[40] Whether to continue the SLCM-N program was an issue in Congress's review and markup of the FY2023 National Defense Authorization Act and FY2023 DOD appropriations act.[41]

Regarding nuclear arms control,[42] GPC was an apparent key factor in connection with the U.S. decision to withdraw from the Intermediate-Range Nuclear Forces (INF) Treaty.[43] The United States has invited China to be a third participant, along with the United States and Russia, in

---

[38] *2022 Nuclear Posture Review*, p. 5. Italics as in original. See also page 11. See also Jonathan Landay and Arshad Mohammed, "US Does Not Need to Boost Nuclear Arsenal to Deter Russia, China," *Reuters*, June 2, 2023.

[39] For an overview, see CRS In Focus IF12084, *Nuclear-Armed Sea-Launched Cruise Missile (SLCM-N)*, by Paul K. Kerr and Mary Beth D. Nikitin.

[40] Regarding the October 2022 NPR, see *2022 Nuclear Posture Review*, pp. 3, 20.

[41] See, for example, Valerie Insinna, "STRATCOM Nominee to 'Assess' Controversial Sea-Launched Nuke Before Cancellation," *Breaking Defense*, September 15, 2022; Kevin Knodell (Honolulu Star-Advertiser), "Congress Quietly Debates New Sea-Based Nuclear Weapons amid China Tensions," *Stars and Stripes*, September 6, 2022; Bill Gertz, "Congress to Restore Nuclear Cruise Missile Funds," *Washington Times*, June 22, 2022; Valerie Insinna, "House Authorizers Approve $45m to Keep Sea-Launched Nuke on Life Support," *Breaking Defense*, June 22, 2022; Mallory Shelbourne and Sam LaGrone, "Lawmakers Question Navy's Decision to Abandon Nuclear Cruise Missile, *USNI News*, June 10 (updated June 11), 2022; Bryant Harris, "US Nuclear Commander Backs Sea-Launched Cruise Missile Biden Would Cancel," *Defense News*, June 7, 2022; Megan Eckstein, "The Navy Doesn't Want Nukes on Ships, Despite Interest from Some Combatant Commanders," *Defense News*, May 13, 2022; John Grady, "Joint Chiefs Vice Chair, STRATCOM CO Still In Favor of Navy Nuclear Cruise Missile," *USNI News*, May 5, 2022; Joe Gould, "US Strategic Command Chief: Sea Missile Cancellation Opens 'Deterrence and Assurance Gap,'" *Defense News*, April 5, 2022; Aaron Mehta, "Milley Breaks with Cancelation of New Nuclear Cruise Missile," *Breaking Defense*, April 5, 2022; Joe Gould, "Biden Plan to Shelve Trump-Era Sea Nuke Comes Under Fire," *Defense News*, April 1, 2022.

[42] For discussions on arms control in the context of GPC, see, for example, Ulrich Kühn and Heather Williams, "A New Approach to Arms Control, How to Safeguard Nuclear Weapons in an Era of Great-Power Politics," *Foreign Affairs*, June 14, 2023; Rebecca K. C. Hersman, Heather Williams, and Suzanne Claeys, *Integrated Arms Control in an Era of Strategic Competition*, CSIS, January 2022, 65 pp.; Jeffrey Lewis, "China Is Radically Expanding Its Nuclear Missile Silos, With More Weapons Likely, It's Time to Go Back to Arms Talks," *Foreign Policy*, June 30, 2021; John Maurer, "Arms Control Among Rivals," American Enterprise Institute, February 11, 2021.

[43] For additional discussion, see CRS Insight IN10985, *U.S. Withdrawal from the INF Treaty*, by Amy F. Woolf.

---

negotiations on future limitations on nuclear arms.[44] China has reportedly refused to join such negotiations,[45] unless the United States agrees to reduce its nuclear forces to China's much-lower level.[46]

On November 16, 2021, following a virtual meeting the previous day between China's President Xi Jinping and President Biden, White House national security advisor Jake Sullivan stated that "the two leaders agreed that we would look to begin to carry forward discussions on strategic stability," and that "it is now incumbent on us to think about the most productive way to carry it forward from here."[47] A November 17, 2021, press report stated

> The United States and China will aim to have 'conversations' on arms control, 'not formal talks', the White House National Security Council said on Wednesday [November 17], downplaying contact on the issue following a meeting between the two countries' leaders.
>
> U.S. President Joe Biden and Chinese leader Xi Jinping agreed this week to "look to begin to carry forward discussions on strategic stability," national security advisor Jake Sullivan said on Tuesday [November 16], in a reference to U.S. concerns about China's nuclear and missile buildup. read more
>
> Following Sullivan's remarks, the NSC cautioned in a statement against "overstating" the status of those conversations, emphasizing that they were not at the same level on which the United States and Russia have engaged for decades.
>
> "It should be clear, as National Security Advisor Sullivan said, this is not the same as the talks we have with Russia, which are mature and have history," an NSC spokesman said.
>
> "These are not arms control talks, but rather conversations with empowered interlocuters," he said without giving details on the format for future contact on the matter.[48]

---

[44] See, for example, Julian E. Barnes and David E. Sanger, "U.S. Will Try to Bring China Into Arms Control Talks," *New York Times*, June 2, 2023; Jack Detsch, "Trump Wants China on Board With New Arms Control Pact," *Foreign Policy*, July 23, 2020; Jeff Mason, Arshad Mohammed, Vladimir Soldatkin, and Andrew Osborne, "Trump Stresses Desire for Arms Control with Russia, China in Putin Call," *Reuters*, May 7, 2020; Emma Farge, "U.S. Urges China to Join Nuclear Arms Talks with Russia," *Reuters*, January 21, 2020; Michael R. Gordon, "U.S. Invites China for Talks on Nuclear Arms," *Wall Street Journal*, December 20, 2019; David Wainter, "Chinese Nuclear Stockpile Clouds Prospects for U.S.-Russia Deal," *Bloomberg*, October 18, 2019. See also Christian Le Miere, "How China Can Benefit from Joining US, Russia in Nuclear Arms Talks," *South China Morning Post*, July 9, 2021.

[45] See, for example, Jay Solomon, "China Rejects Nuclear Talks with the U.S. As It Looks to Strengthen Its Own Arsenal," *Semafor*, June 9, 2023; Kathrin Hille, "US and China Are Not Ready to Talk About Nuclear Arms Controls, China Wants to Tackle Growing Risk of Nuclear Conflict but Is Reluctant to Curb Its Nuclear Weapons Programme," *Financial Times*, January 11, 2022; Emma Frage, "U.S. Says China Is Resisting Nuclear Arms Talks," *Reuters*, May 18, 2021; John Dotson, "Beijing Rejects Any Involvement in Nuclear Arms Limitation Talks," Jamestown Foundation, October 30, 2020; Associated Press, "China Calls US Invite to Nuclear Talks a Ploy to Derail Them," *Associated Press*, July 8, 2020; Robbie Gramer and Jack Detsch, "Trump Fixates on China as Nuclear Arms Pact Nears Expiration," *Foreign Policy*, April 29, 2020; Hal Brands, "China Has No Reason to Make a Deal on Nuclear Weapons," *Bloomberg*, April 29, 2020; Cheng Hanping, "US Attempt to Rope China into New START Negotiations Won't Succeed," *Global Times*, February 12, 2020; Steven Pifer, "Trump's Bid to Go Big on Nuclear Arms Looks Like a Fizzle," *Defense One*, February 5, 2020; Samuel Osborne, "China Refuses to Join Nuclear Talks with US and Russia in Blow for Trump," *Independent (UK)*, May 7, 2019; Ben Blanchard, "China Says It Won't Take Part in Trilateral Nuclear Arms Talks," *Reuters*, May 6, 2019; Ben Westcott, "China 'Will Not Participate' in Trump's Proposed Three-Way Nuclear Talks, CNN, May 6, 2019.

[46] See, for example, Yew Lun Tian, "China Challenges U.S. to Cut Nuclear Arsenal to Matching Level," *Reuters*, July 7, 2020.

[47] As quoted in Alex Leary, Lingling Wei, and Michael R. Gordon, "Biden, Xi Open to Nuclear-Arms Talks, White House Says," *Wall Street Journal*, November 16, 2021. See also Patrick Tucker, "Biden Launches Arms-Control Talks with China, Warns Xi on Taiwan," *Defense One*, November 16, 2021.

[48] Michael Martina and David Brunnstrom, "U.S. Says It Is Not Engaged in Formal Arms Control Talks with China," (continued...)

A February 25, 2022, blog post stated: "The Biden administration has cut off arms control talks with Russia, sources familiar with the decision told Foreign Policy. The move came after Russian President Vladimir Putin sent troops into Ukraine's breakaway regions but before he launched the full-scale invasion of the country."[49]

A November 1, 2022, press report stated that

> China has shown no interest in discussing steps to reduce the risk posed by nuclear weapons, senior U.S. officials said on Tuesday [November 1]....
>
> Alexandra Bell, deputy assistant secretary of state for arms control, verification and compliance, told an Atlantic Council [forum] that despite U.S. efforts, Washington and Beijing still had not begun engagement on the issue....
>
> Richard Johnson, the U.S. deputy assistant secretary of defense for Nuclear and Countering Weapons of Mass Destruction Policy, told the forum the United States was looking to begin exchanges with China on "more basic things" than the number of warheads.
>
> "If that's the argument that Beijing is giving, we're not asking to have a discussion about numbers. We're saying, let's talk about putting some guardrails into the relationship so that we don't have unnecessary crises," he said.
>
> Johnson added that if Beijing preferred to not engage bilaterally, it could "demonstrate some transparency" about its nuclear build-up through the International Atomic Energy Agency by declaring its plutonium stocks for civilian purposes.
>
> "The Chinese have stopped doing that, and that's a real concern," he said.[50]

Global U.S. Military Posture

Overview

The emergence of GPC has led to increased discussion about global U.S. military posture, including discussion regarding

- the portion of U.S. forces that are forward-deployed to distant regions on a sustained basis for purposes such as deterring potential regional aggressors, reassuring allies and partners, and rapidly responding to crises; and

- the day-to-day global distribution of U.S. military capabilities and force deployments across regions such as the Indo-Pacific (for countering Chinese and North Korean military capabilities), Europe (for countering Russian military capabilities), the Middle East (for countering Iranian military capabilities and addressing other security concerns), and other regions (such as Africa, Latin America, and the Arctic).

Reuters, November 17, 2021. See also David E. Sanger and William J. Broad, "As China Speeds Up Nuclear Arms Race, the U.S. Wants to Talk," *New York Times*, November 28, 2021; Chao Deng and Alastair Gale, "U.S. Pushes Arms-Control Talks as China's Nuclear Arsenal Grows," *Wall Street Journal*, November 18, 2021; Demetri Sevastopulo and Tom Mitchell, "Xi-Biden agreement on nuclear talks clouded by 'deep distrust,'" *Financial Times*, November 17, 2021; Demetri Sevastopulo and Tom Mitchell, "US and China Agree to Hold Talks on Nuclear Arsenals," *Financial Times*, November 16, 2021.

[49] Jack Detsch and Robbie Gramer, "Biden Halts Russian Arms Control Talks Amid Ukraine Invasion," *Foreign Policy*, February 25, 2022. See also Peter Huessy, "Have Russia and China Killed Nuclear Arms Control?" *National Interest*, February 20, 2022.

[50] Michael Martina and David Brunnstrom, "U.S. Says China Resisting Nuclear Talks after Xi Vow to Boost Deterrent," *Reuters*, November 1, 2022.

The benefits, costs, and risks of forward-deploying U.S. forces to distant regions on a sustained basis rather than basing them in the United States and deploying them to distant regions in response to specific contingencies is a long-standing issue in U.S. defense planning.[51]

Regarding the regional distribution of U.S. military capabilities and force deployments, U.S. officials since at least 2006 have expressed desires (or announced plans) for bolstering U.S. military capabilities and force deployments in the Indo-Pacific region so as to counter China's growing military capabilities. On the other hand, Russia's actions in Europe and developments in the Middle East pose their own security challenges, and some observers express concern about a scenario in which the United States could face major military contingencies in multiple parts of Eurasia in rapid succession or simultaneously[52]—a consideration that can complicate plans for shifting U.S. military capabilities from Europe or the Middle East to the Indo-Pacific.

Key issues observers are debating include how much priority U.S. defense planning should give to Europe (to deter or respond to Russian actions) versus the Indo-Pacific (to deter China);[53] how the U.S. response to Russia's invasion of multiple parts of Ukraine starting on February 24, 2022, might influence China's calculations regarding potential actions it might take toward Taiwan; and whether the tension about how to address concerns about both China and Russia should lead to changes in U.S. grand strategy or defense strategy and/or the size of the U.S. defense budget.[54]

---

[51] See, for example, Billy Fabian, "Overcoming the Tyranny of Time: The Role of U.S. Forward Posture in Deterrence and Defense," CSIS, September 21, 2020. As another example, see CRS In Focus IF11280, *U.S. Military Presence in Poland*, by Andrew Feickert, Kathleen J. McInnis, and Derek E. Mix.

[52] See, for example, Thomas G. Mahnken, "Could America Win a New World War? What It Would Take to Defeat Both China and Russia," *Foreign Affairs*, October 27, 2022; Hal Brands, "Can the US Take on China, Iran and Russia All at Once?" *Bloomberg*, October 16, 2022; Sebastian Sprenger and Joe Gould, "US Military Readies to 'Walk and Chew Gum' as Multiple Crises Loom," *Defense News*, January 28, 2022.

[53] See, for example, Luis Simón and Zack Cooper, "Rethinking Tradeoffs between Europe and the Indo-Pacific," *War on the Rocks*, May 9, 2023.

[54] See, for example, Hal Brands, "Ukraine's Survival Is Vital to Japan, South Korea and Taiwan," *Bloomberg*, June 1, 2023; Robert D. Blackwill and Richard Fontaine, "Ukraine War Should Slow But Not Stop the U.S. Pivot to Asia," *Bloomberg*, March 8, 2022; John Ferrari, "Tear Up the National Defense Strategy and Start Again, Recognizing Reality," *Breaking Defense*, March 8, 2022; Editorial Board, "Rebuilding U.S. Defenses After Ukraine, Biden Needs to Pivot to Meet Growing Threats as Jimmy Carter Did," *Wall Street Journal*, March 7, 2022; Catie Edmondson, "War in Ukraine Rallies Support in Congress for More Military Spending," *New York Times*, March 7, 2022; Glenn Hubbard, "NATO Needs More Guns and Less Butter, Russia's Invasion of Ukraine Will Require a Jolting Shift in the West's Spending Priorities," *Wall Street Journal*, March 7, 2022; Thomas Spoehr, "The Biden Administration Needs to get Serious About National Defense," *Newsweek*, March 7, 2022; Bradley Thayer, "Russia's War In Ukraine: A Balance Of Power Problem For America?" *19FortyFive*, March 7, 2022; Sebastian Sprenger, Joe Gould, Vivienne Machi, and Tom Kington, "Stunned by Putin's War, Nations Rewrite Their Playbooks on Defense," *Defense News*, March 4, 2022; Robert M. Gates, "We Need a More Realistic Strategy for the Post-Cold War Era," *Washington Post*, March 3, 2022; Connor O'Brien, Paul McLeary, and Lee Hudson, "Russia Crisis Forces Pentagon to Rework Defense Strategy on the Fly," *Politico Pro*, March 3 (updated March 4), 2022; John Ferrari and Elaine McCusker, "The Ukraine Invasion Shows Why America Needs to Get Its Defense Budget in Order," *Breaking Defense*, March 2, 2022; Tony Bertuca, "DOD official: New National Defense Strategy Will Keep China First, But Reflect New Reality with Russia," *Inside Defense*, February 28, 2022; Mackenzie Eaglen, "How the Ukraine Crisis Could Make the US Military Stronger," American Enterprise Institute, March 1, 2022; Joe Gould, "Pentagon Revisiting Long-Term US Troop Levels in Eastern Europe," *Defense News*, March 1, 2022; John M. Donnelly, "Russian Threat Is Forcing a Rewrite of US Defense Plans," *CQ*, February 25, 2022; Raphael S. Cohen, "The False Choice Between China and Russia," *The Hill*, February 21, 2022; Matthew Kroenig, "Washington Must Prepare for War With Both Russia and China, Pivoting to Asia and Forgetting About Europe Isn't an Option," *Foreign Policy*, February 18, 2022; Michael J. Green, and Gabriel Scheinmann, "Even an 'Asia First' Strategy Needs to Deter Russia in Ukraine, There Is No Indo-Pacific Strategy Without U.S. Pushback Against Russia," *Foreign Policy*, February 17, 2022; Barry Pavel, "Biden Should Shift US Troop Positions Worldwide, The Crisis in Europe Makes Clear that Biden's Team Should Rethink Their First National Defense Strategy, Quickly," *Defense One*, February 17, 2022; John Bolton, "Entente Multiplies the Threat From Russia (continued...)

Obama Administration Strategic Rebalancing (Strategic Pivot) to Asia-Pacific

The Obama Administration, as part of an initiative it referred to as strategic rebalancing or the strategic pivot, sought to reduce U.S. force deployments in Iraq and Afghanistan, in part to facilitate an increase in U.S. force deployments to the Asia-Pacific region for countering China.[55]

Trump Administration Planned Actions

The Trump Administration stated that a reduction of U.S. military personnel in Germany that it planned was intended, at least in part, to facilitate a reallocation of additional U.S. forces to the Indo-Pacific region.[56] In addition, President Trump expressed a desire to reduce U.S. military deployments to the Middle East, and Trump Administration officials stated that the Administration was considering reducing U.S. military deployments to Africa and South America, in part to facilitate an increase in U.S. force deployments to the Indo-Pacific region for countering China.[57] The Trump Administration's proposals for reducing force deployments to Africa and South America became a subject of debate, in part because they were viewed by some observers as creating a risk of leading to increased Chinese or Russian influence in those regions.[58]

---

and China, The Misguided Idea that the U.S. Needs to Ignore One to Focus on the Other Intensifies the Danger," *Wall Street Journal*, February 15, 2022; Walter Russell Mead, "'Asia First' Misses the Point, The U.S. Needs a Coherent Strategy for Both Security and Economic Policy," *Wall Street Journal*, February 14, 2022; Elbridge Colby and Oriana Skylar Mastro, "Ukraine Is a Distraction From Taiwan, Getting Bogged Down in Europe Will Impede the U.S.'s Ability to Compete with China in the Pacific," *Wall Street Journal*, February 13, 2022; Ashley Townshend, "U.S. Indo-Pacific Power Depends on Restraint in Ukraine, Washington Must Reassure Quad Partners That It Won't Be Distracted in Europe," *Foreign Policy*, February 9, 2022; Walter Russell Mead, "Time to Increase Defense Spending, The U.S. Will Face Challenges from the New Alliance between China and Russia," *Wall Street Journal*, February 7, 2022; Seth Cropsey, "Double-Down on the Indo-Pacific in the Midst of a Ukraine Crisis," *The Hill*, February 1, 2022; Dov S. Zakheim, "The Biden Administration Faces a Dangerous Anti-American Triad," *The Hill*, January 28, 2022; Josh Rogin, "Putin Is Threatening to Wreck Biden's Asia Strategy," *Washington Post*, January 27, 2022; Simon Jackman, "Putin Tries to Trump Indo-Pacific," United States Studies Centre, January 26, 2022. See also some of the articles dated from January 2022 onward that are listed in **Appendix C**.

[55] For more on the Obama Administration's strategic rebalancing initiative, which included political and economic dimensions as well as planned military force redeployments, see CRS Report R42448, *Pivot to the Pacific? The Obama Administration's "Rebalancing" Toward Asia*, coordinated by Mark E. Manyin, and CRS In Focus IF10029, *China, U.S. Leadership, and Geopolitical Challenges in Asia*, by Susan V. Lawrence.

[56] Robert C. O'Brien, "Why the U.S. Is Moving Troops Out of Germany, Forces Are Needed in the Indo-Pacific. And Berlin Should Contribute More to European Security," *Wall Street Journal*, June 21, 2020; Jamie McIntyre, "Polish Leader Leaves with No New Commitment of US Troops as Pentagon Shifts Focus Away from Europe and Toward Countering China," *Washington Examiner*, June 25, 2020; Tsuyoshi Nagasawa and Shotaro Miyasaka, "Thousands of US Troops Will Shift to Asia-Pacific to Guard Against China, German Contingent to Redeploy to Guam, Hawaii, Alaska, Japan and Australia," *Nikkei Asian Review*, July 5, 2020. See also CRS In Focus IF11280, *U.S. Military Presence in Poland*, by Andrew Feickert, Kathleen J. McInnis, and Derek E. Mix.

[57] See, for example, Glen Carey, "U.S. Pentagon Chief Wants to Reallocate Forces to Indo-Pacific," *Bloomberg*, December 7, 2019; Shawn Snow, "Esper Wants to Move Troops from Afghanistan to the Indo-Pacific to Confront China," *Military Times*, December 18, 2019; Helene Cooper, Thomas Gibbons-Neff, and Eric Schmitt, "Pentagon Eyes Africa Drawdown as First Step in Global Troop Shift," *New York Times*, December 24, 2019, Robert Burns, "Pentagon Sees Taliban Deal as Allowing Fuller Focus on China," *Associated Press*, March 1, 2020. See also Kyle Rempfer, "Soldiers Will Spend Longer Deployments in Asia," *Army Times*, February 20, 2020; Mike Sweeney, "Considering the 'Zero Option,' Cold War Lessons on U.S. Basing in the Middle East," Defense Priorities, March 2020.

[58] See, for example, Scott D. Adamson, "Don't Discount America's Interest in Keeping Africa Safe," *Defense One*, December 21, 2020; Diana Stancy Correll, "Lawmakers Voice Concern About a Potential Troop Reduction in Africa," *Military Times*, January 14, 2020; Joe Gould, "Esper's Africa Drawdown Snags on Capitol Hill," *Defense News*, January 16, 2020; Ellen Mitchell, "Lawmakers Push Back at Pentagon's Possible Africa Drawdown," *The Hill*, January 19, 2020; K. Riva Levinson, "Broad, Bipartisan Rebuke for Proposal to Pull Troops from Africa," *The Hill*, January 21, 2020; Carley Petesch (Associated Press), "Allies Worry as US Ponders Cutting Military Forces in Africa," *Military* (continued...)

Biden Administration Global Posture Review

On February 4, 2021, President Biden announced that "Defense Secretary Austin will be leading a Global Posture Review of our forces so that our military footprint is appropriately aligned with our foreign policy and national security priorities."[59] A DOD news report the next day that

> The global posture review will examine the U.S. military's footprint, resources and strategies. "This review will help inform the secretary's advice to the commander-in-chief about how we best allocate military forces in pursuit of our national interests," [Pentagon Press Secretary John F.] Kirby said.
>
> The global posture review will be led by the acting undersecretary of defense for policy in close coordination with the chairman of the Joint Chiefs of Staff.
>
> U.S. officials will consult often with allies and partners around the world as they perform the review, Kirby said. The review should be finished by mid-year.
>
> The review will use American defense strategy and look where service members are based, and if this is the best place to be based. This will, of course, take into consideration any treaty or agreement. Commitments—like the rotational forces in Poland and Korea—will be considered and those deployments will continue even as the review goes on. President Biden said the movement of U.S. forces from Germany will stop until the review is completed.
>
> It is not just forward-deployed land or air forces that will be considered. Naval forces and where they operate will be part of the equation, Kirby said.[60]

On November 29, 2021, DOD announced that

> President Joe Biden has accepted the recommendations formed by Secretary of Defense Lloyd J. Austin III on the global posture review, Mara Karlin, performing the duties of deputy undersecretary of defense for policy, announced today....
>
> It is no surprise that the Indo-Pacific is the priority region for the review, given the secretary's focus on China as America's pacing challenge. The review directs additional

---

Times, January 29, 2020; Lara Seligman and Robbie Gramer, "Pentagon Debates Drawdown in Africa, South America," *Foreign Policy*, January 30, 2020; "Jacqueline Feldscher, "Esper Says Troop Presence in Africa, South America Could Grow," *Politico Pro*, January 30, 2020; Joe Gould, "Expect Congress to Block Africa Troop Cuts, Says Defense Panel Chairman," *Defense News*, February 27, 2020; Eric Schmitt, "Terrorism Threat in West Africa Soars as U.S. Weighs Troop Cuts," *New York Times*, February 27, 2020; Matthew Dalton, "The US Should Send More, Not Fewer, Troops to West Africa," *Defense One*, March 3, 2020; Robbie Gramer, "U.S. Congress Moves to Restrain Pentagon Over Africa Drawdown Plans," *Foreign Policy*, March 4, 2020; Sam Wilkins, "Does America Need an Africa Strategy?" *War on the Rocks*, April 2, 2020; Herman J. Cohen, "Pulling Troops Out of Africa Could Mean Another Endless War," *War on the Rocks*, May 13, 2020; Samuel Ramani, "France and the United States Are Making West Africa's Security Situation Worse, France's Unilateralism and the United States' Wavering Are Destabilizing the Sahel—and Creating An Opening for Russia and China," *Foreign Policy*, September 12, 2020; John Turner, "In America's Absence, China Is Taking Latin America By Storm," *National Interest*, September 21, 2020; Will Reno and Jesse Humpal, "As the US Slumps Away, China Subsumes African Security Arrangements," *Defense One*, October 21, 2020; Warren P. Strobel and Gordon Lubold, "Pentagon Draw-Down at U.S. Embassies Prompts Concern About Ceding Field to Global Rivals," *Wall Street Journal*, November 1, 2020; Samuel Ramani, "Trump's Plan to Withdraw From Somalia Couldn't Come at a Worse Time," *Foreign Policy*, November 2, 2020.

[59] White House, "Remarks by President Biden on America's Place in the World," February 4, 2021.

[60] Jim Garamone, "Global Posture Review Will Tie Strategy, Defense Policy to Basing," *DOD News*, February 5, 2021. See also Lolita C. Baldor, "Biden Halts Trump-Ordered US Troops Cuts in Germany," *Associated Press*, February 4, 2021; Ed Adamczyk, "Defense Secretary Austin Announces Global Force Posture Review," *United Press International*, February 5, 2021; Robert Burns, "Pentagon Rethinking How to Array Forces to Focus on China," *Associated Press*, February 17, 2021; Christopher Woody, "Biden Wants the Military's Footprint to be 'Correctly Sized,' and It May Mean Deciding Which Bases Really Matter," *Business Insider*, March 18, 2021.

---

cooperation with allies and partners to advance initiatives that contribute to regional stability and deter Chinese military aggression and threats from North Korea, Karlin said.

These initiatives include seeking greater regional access for military partnership activities, enhancing infrastructure in Guam and Australia and prioritizing military construction across the Pacific Islands. They also include new U.S. rotational aircraft deployments and logistics cooperation in Australia, which DOD announced in September.

The review also approved the stationing of a previously rotational attack helicopter squadron and an artillery division headquarters in the Republic of Korea.

More initiatives are forthcoming in the region, but these require more discussions among the allies and remain classified, Karlin said.

In Europe, the review looks to strengthen the U.S. combat deterrent against Russia, and enable NATO forces to operate more effectively, she said. DOD has already instituted a couple of recommendations including lifting the 25,000-man cap on active duty troops in Germany imposed by the previous administration and the decision to permanently base a multi-domain task force and theater fires command—a total of 500 U.S. Army personnel—in Wiesbaden, Germany. DOD will also retain seven sites previously designated for return to Germany and Belgium under the European infrastructure consolidation plan. The review identified additional capabilities that will enhance U.S. deterrence posture in Europe, and these will be discussed with allies in the near future, Karlin said.

In the Middle East, again, there have already been some posture review changes including the redeployment of critically strained missile defense capabilities, and reallocation of certain maritime assets back to Europe and the Indo-Pacific. In Iraq and Syria, the review indicates that DOD posture will continue to support the defeated Islamic State campaign and build the capacity of partner forces, Karlin said.

"Looking ahead, the global posture review directs the department to conduct an additional analysis on enduring posture requirements in the Middle East," she said. "As Secretary Austin noted … we have global responsibilities and must ensure the readiness and modernization of our forces. These considerations require us to make continuous changes to our Middle East posture, but we always have the capability to rapidly deploy forces to the region based on the threat environment."

In considering forces in Africa, analysis from the review supports several ongoing interagency reviews to ensure DOD has an appropriately scoped posture to monitor threats from regional violent extremist organizations, support American diplomatic activities and enable allies and partners, according to the official.

Finally, in Central and South America and the Caribbean, the review looks at DOD posture in support of national security objectives, including humanitarian assistance, disaster relief and counterdrug missions. "The GPR directs that DOD posture continue to support U.S. government efforts on the range of transnational challenges and to add to defense partnership activities in the region," the official said.[61]

Details on the results of the global posture review are largely classified.[62] One press report stated that the review "plans to make improvements to airfields in Guam and Australia to counter China but contains no major reshuffling of forces as the U.S. moves to take on Beijing while deterring Russia and fighting terrorism in the Middle East and Africa."[63] Some observers criticized the

---

[61] Jim Garamone, "Biden Approves Global Posture Review Recommendations," *DOD Ne*ws, November 29, 2021.

[62] See, for example, Meghann Myers, "Pentagon's Military Presence Review Done, but Details Lacking on New Deployments, Troop Plus-Ups or Home-Port Shifts," *Military Times*, November 29, 2021.

[63] Gordon Lubold, "Pentagon Plans to Improve Airfields in Guam and Australia to Confront China," *Wall Street Journal*, November 29, 2021.

review for apparently not recommending larger-scale changes, particularly for strengthening U.S. posture in the Indo-Pacific region for countering China.[64]

Russia's Invasion of Ukraine Complicates Plans for Shift to Indo-Pacific

As mentioned above, Russia's invasion of multiple parts of Ukraine starting on February 24, 2022, has prompted increased discussion of how much priority U.S. defense planning should give to Europe (to deter and respond to Russian actions) versus the Indo-Pacific (to deter China), how the U.S. response to Russia's actions in Ukraine might influence China's calculations regarding potential actions it might take toward Taiwan, and whether the tension about how to address concerns about both China and Russia should lead to changes in U.S. grand strategy or defense strategy, and/or the size of the U.S. defense budget.[65]

Discussions within NATO about the so-called burden-sharing issue—which focuses on comparisons of U.S. versus allied contributions toward the common defense of NATO—have often centered to a large degree on U.S. concerns about equity within the alliance and whether some of the NATO allies are free riding within the alliance.[66] In a context of GPC, and particularly in light of Russia's invasion of multiple parts of Ukraine starting on February 24, 2022, discussions about whether NATO allies should increase their contributions toward the common defense of NATO could additionally focus on a question of compensating for potential limits on U.S. defense resources that are available for Europe.[67] The announced strategic partnership between China and Russia has led some U.S. observers to argue that avoiding unwanted tradeoffs between U.S. military investments for countering China and those for countering Russia could require increasing U.S. defense spending above current levels.[68]

Developments in Middle East Complicate Plans for Shift to Indo-Pacific

Developments in the Middle East affecting U.S. interests are viewed as complicating plans or desires that U.S. leaders might have for reducing U.S. force deployments to that region so as to

---

[64] See, for example, Stacie L. Pettyjohn, "Spiking the Problem: Developing a Resilient Posture in the Indo-Pacific with Passive Defenses," *War on the Rocks*, January 10, 2022; Becca Wasser, "The Unmet Promise of the Global Posture Review," *War on the Rocks*, December 30, 2021; Dakota Wood, "Joe Biden's Global Posture Review Was a Nothingburger," Heritage Foundation, December 13, 2021; Dov S. Zakheim, "A Disappointing Global Posture Review from Defense," *The Hill*, December 3, 2021; Jack Detsch, "'No Decisions, No Changes': Pentagon Fails to Stick Asia Pivot, The Long-Anticipated Review Was, for Some, a 'Complete Waste of time.'" *Foreign Policy*, November 29, 2021; Editorial Board, "The Pentagon's Bureaucratic Posture Review," *Wall Street Journal*, December 1, 2021; Daniel DePetris, "Biden's Pentagon Wants to Keep the Military Overstretched," *Spectator World*, November 30, 2021. See also Kelley Beaucar Vlahos, "Pentagon: U.S. Military Footprint Staying Right Where It Is," *Responsible Statecraft*, November 30, 2021.

[65] See the sources cited in footnote 54.

[66] See, for example, Emma Ashford and Matthew Kroenig, "Is Europe Serious About Self-Defense, or Free-Riding?" *Foreign Policy*, June 2, 2023.

[67] If observers assess that, in light of finite U.S. defense resources and the scale of the security challenge posed in the Indo-Pacific by China's growing military capabilities, the United States might not have sufficient resources to adequately counter China's growing military capabilities while at the same time maintaining historic U.S. levels of investment for countering Russian forces in Europe, then adequately countering China could require reducing U.S. expenditures for countering Russia, which in turn could require NATO allies to compensate by increasing their own investments within the NATO alliance for countering Russia. See, for example, Robert Kelly, "America's Great Security Challenge Is China. Why Can't Europe Handle Ukraine?" *19FortyFive*, February 7, 2022; Dov S. Zakheim, "The Biden Administration Faces a Dangerous Anti-American Triad," *The Hill*, January 28, 2022.

[68] See the sources cited in footnote 54.

---

make them available for deployment elsewhere.[69] In April and June 2021, it was reported that the Biden Administration had decided to withdraw certain U.S. forces, including fighter squadrons and Patriot and THAAD (Terminal High Altitude Area Defense) missile defense batteries, from the Middle East, so that some of them could be redeployed elsewhere.[70]

U.S. and Allied Capabilities in Indo-Pacific Region

The emergence of GPC with China has led to a major U.S. defense-planning focus on strengthening U.S. military capabilities in the Indo-Pacific region. U.S. officials since 2006 have expressed desires (or announced plans) for bolstering U.S. military capabilities and force deployments in the Indo-Pacific region for the purpose of countering China's growing military capabilities. Strengthening U.S. military capabilities in the Indo-Pacific is a key component of the Free and Open Indo-Pacific (FOIP), an overarching U.S. policy construct for the region that emerged during the Trump Administration[71] and has continued during the Biden Administration.[72] As mentioned earlier, the Biden Administration's October 2022 NDS states that DOD's priorities include "Deterring aggression, while being prepared to prevail in conflict when necessary— prioritizing the PRC challenge in the Indo-Pacific region, then the Russia challenge in Europe."[73] The NDS also states

> *The Indo-Pacific Region.* The Department will reinforce and build out a resilient security architecture in the Indo-Pacific region in order to sustain a free and open regional order, and deter attempts to resolve disputes by force. We will modernize our Alliance with Japan and strengthen combined capabilities by aligning strategic planning and priorities in a more

---

[69] See, for example, Jon B. Alterman, "A U.S. Pivot Away from the Middle East: Fact or Fiction?" Center for Strategic and International Studies (CSIS), May 23, 2023; Michael R. Gordon, Dion Nissenbaum, and Jared Malsin, "Mideast Challenges Mount for U.S. as Its Forces Come Under Renewed Fire, The Middle East's Shifting Geopolitics, Coming amid Gains by China and Russia, Are Complicating Washington's Plans in the Region," *Wall Street Journal*, March 25, 2023; Michael R. Gordon, "U.S. to Send Aging Attack Planes to Mideast and Shift Newer Jets to Asia, Europe, As Stretched Military Moves Toward 'Great Power' Competition with China and Russia, It Looks to Avoid Shortfall in Middle East," *Wall Street Journal*, March 23, 2023; Walter Russell Mead, "The Peril of Ignoring the Middle East," *Wall Street Journal*, January 9, 2023; Jon B. Alterman, "The Middle East's Coming Centrality," CSIS, September 20, 2022; Danielle Pletka, "The U.S. Can't Just Quit the Middle East, We Have Genuine Geopolitical Interests in the Region, and So We Must Repair the Relationships We've Damaged," *Dispatch*, March 30, 2022; Saeed Ghasseminejad, "Is the Future of the Persian Gulf Chinese?" *National Interest*, February 2, 2022; Edward White and Andrew England, "China Pours Money into Iraq as US Retreats from Middle East," *Financial Times*, February 2, 2022; Ben Hubbard and Amy Qin, "As the U.S. Pulls Back From the Mideast, China Leans In," *New York Times*, February 1 (updated February 2), 2022; Jane Arraf and Ben Hubbard, "As Islamic State Resurges, U.S. Is Drawn Back Into the Fray," *New York Times*, January 25, 2022; Bradley Bowman, "Biden Can No Longer Ignore Growing Iran-China Ties, Washington May Be Tired of the Middle East, But Beijing Is Just Getting Started," *Foreign Policy*, January 13, 2022.

[70] See Gordon Lubold and Warren P. Strobel, "Biden Trimming Forces Sent to Mideast to Help Saudi Arabia," *Wall Street Journal*, April 1, 2021; Oren Liebermann, "Pentagon Pulls Missile Defense, Other Systems from Saudi Arabia and Other Middle East Countries," *CNN*, June 18, 2021; Gordon Lubold, Nancy A. Youssef, and Michael R. Gordon, "U.S. Military to Withdraw Hundreds of Troops, Aircraft, Antimissile Batteries From Middle East," *Wall Street Journal*, June 18, 2021; Stephen Losey, "US to Pull Some Patriot Missile Batteries, Fighter Squadrons Out of Middle East," *Military.com*, June 21, 2021.

[71] See CRS Report R45396, *The Trump Administration's "Free and Open Indo-Pacific": Issues for Congress*, coordinated by Bruce Vaughn; and CRS Report R46217, *Indo-Pacific Strategies of U.S. Allies and Partners: Issues for Congress*, coordinated by Ben Dolven and Bruce Vaughn. See also White House, "President Donald J. Trump's Administration Is Advancing a Free and Open Indo-Pacific," July 20, 2018, Department of State, "Advancing a Free and Open Indo-Pacific," July 30, 2018, Department of State, "Briefing on the Indo-Pacific Strategy," April 2, 2018, Department of State, "Remarks on 'America's Indo-Pacific Economic Vision,'" remarks by Secretary of State Michael R. Pompeo, Indo-Pacific Business Forum, U.S. Chamber of Commerce, Washington, DC, July 30, 2018.

[72] See, for example, White House, *National Security Strategy*, October 2022, pp. 37-38.

[73] Department of Defense, *2022 National Defense Strategy of the United States of America*, cover letter dated October 27, 2022, p. 7.

---

integrated manner; deepen our Alliance with Australia through investments in posture, interoperability, and expansion of multilateral cooperation; and foster advantage through advanced technology cooperation with partnerships like AUKUS and the Indo-Pacific Quad. The Department will advance our Major Defense Partnership with India to enhance its ability to deter PRC aggression and ensure free and open access to the Indian Ocean region. The Department will support Taiwan's asymmetric self-defense commensurate with the evolving PRC threat and consistent with our one China policy. We will work with the ROK to continue to improve its defense capability to lead the Alliance combined defense, with U.S. forces augmenting those of the ROK. We will invigorate multilateral approaches to security challenges in the region, to include by promoting the role of the Association of Southeast Asian Nations in addressing regional security issues. The Department will work with Allies and partners to ensure power projection in a contested environment. The Department will also support Ally and partner efforts, in accordance with U.S. policy and international law, to address acute forms of gray zone coercion from the PRC's campaigns to establish control over the East China Sea, Taiwan Strait, South China Sea, and disputed land borders such as with India. At the same time, the Department will continue to prioritize maintaining open lines of communication with the PLA and managing competition responsibly.[74]

In discussions about strengthening U.S. military capabilities in the Indo-Pacific region for countering China, actual or potential U.S. measures that are frequently mentioned include

- shifting to more distributed force architectures;[75]

- shifting to new operational concepts (i.e., ways of employing military forces) that are more distributed, make greater use of unmanned vehicles, and employ a higher degree of integration of operating domains (i.e., space, cyberspace, air, land, sea, and undersea);

- increasing numbers of longer-ranged aircraft and missiles;

- hardening air bases and other facilities in the Indo-Pacific that are within range of Chinese weapons;

- exploiting areas (such as undersea warfare) where the United States has an advantage that China cannot quickly overcome; and

- making U.S. C4ISR (command, control, communications, computers, intelligence, surveillance, and reconnaissance) and logistics capabilities more resilient against attack by Chinese weapons, and more quickly reconstitutable.

As one service-oriented example of DOD actions to strengthen U.S. military capabilities in the Indo-Pacific, the Navy has shifted a greater part of its fleet to the region; is assigning its most capable new ships and aircraft and its best personnel to the Pacific; is maintaining or increasing general presence operations, training and developmental exercises, and engagement and cooperation with allied and other navies in the Indo-Pacific; has increased the planned future size of the Navy; has initiated, increased, or accelerated numerous programs for developing new military technologies and acquiring new ships, aircraft, unmanned vehicles, and weapons; is developing new operational concepts; and has signaled that the Navy in coming years will shift to

---

[74] Department of Defense, *2022 National Defense Strategy of the United States of America*, cover letter dated October 27, 2022, pp. 14-15.

[75] In general, more distributed force architectures would include a smaller portion of larger and individually more expensive platforms (such as larger ships) and a larger proportion of smaller and individually less expensive platforms, including unmanned vehicles. A primary aim in shifting a force to a more distributed architecture is to reduce the force's vulnerability to attack by complicating the adversary's task of detecting, identifying, and tracking the force's components and avoiding a situation of having "too many eggs in one basket."

a more distributed fleet architecture.[76] As another example, the Marine Corps' current plan to redesign its forces, called Force Design 2030, is driven primarily by a need to better prepare the Marine Corps for potential operations against Chinese forces in a conflict in the Western Pacific.[77]

Day-to-day DOD activities in the Indo-Pacific region include those for competing strategically with China in the South and East China Seas.[78] They also include numerous activities to help strengthen the military capabilities of U.S. allies in the region, particularly Japan and Australia, and also South Korea, the Philippines, and New Zealand, as well as activities to improve the ability of forces from these countries to operate effectively with U.S. forces (referred to as military interoperability) and activities to improve the military capabilities of emerging security partners in the region, such as Vietnam.

Much of the conversation about strengthening U.S. military capabilities in the Indo-Pacific region revolves around the Pacific Deterrence Initiative (PDI), which is a term used to refer to a collection of DOD investments that DOD officials and policymakers have identified as important for bolstering U.S. military capabilities in the region. The PDI is broadly modeled after the European Deterrence Initiative (or EDI—see the next section). Some PDI items are new initiatives, while others are existing DOD programs that have been brought under the PDI rubric. Some have been funded or are requested for funding in the Administration's proposed defense budget, while others have not yet been funded or had funding requested for them in the Administration's proposed budget (but might have been included in DOD's unfunded priority lists [UPLs]).[79]

---

[76] For additional discussion, see CRS Report RL33153, *China Naval Modernization: Implications for U.S. Navy Capabilities—Background and Issues for Congress*, by Ronald O'Rourke.

[77] For additional discussion, see CRS Insight IN11281, *New U.S. Marine Corps Force Design Initiative: Force Design 2030*, by Andrew Feickert. See also CRS Report RL32665, *Navy Force Structure and Shipbuilding Plans: Background and Issues for Congress*, by Ronald O'Rourke, and CRS Report R46374, *Navy Medium Landing Ship (LSM) (Previously Light Amphibious Warship [LAW]) Program: Background and Issues for Congress*, by Ronald O'Rourke.

[78] For more on this competition, see CRS Report R42784, *U.S.-China Strategic Competition in South and East China Seas: Background and Issues for Congress*, by Ronald O'Rourke.

[79] UPLs are lists of programs that DOD officials submit to Congress in conjunction with each year's defense budget submission to show what additional programs those officials would like to see funded, if additional funding could be made available.

Regarding the origin of the PDI, in April 2020, it was reported that Admiral Philip (Phil) Davidson, Commander of U.S. Indo-Pacific Command (INDOPACOM), had submitted to Congress a $20.1 billion plan for investments for improving U.S. military capabilities in the Indo-Pacific region. Davidson submitted the plan, entitled Regain the Advantage, in response to Section 1253 of the FY2020 National Defense Authorization Act (S. 1790/P.L. 116-92 of December 20, 2019), which required the Commander of INDOPACOM to submit to the congressional defense committees a report providing the Commander's independent assessment of the activities and resources required, for FY2022-FY2026, to implement the National Defense Strategy with respect to the Indo-Pacific region, maintain or restore the comparative U.S. military advantage relative to China, and reduce the risk associated with executing DOD contingency plans. Davidson's plan requested about $1.6 billion in additional funding suggestions for FY2021 above what the Pentagon was requesting in its proposed FY2021 budget, and about $18.5 billion in investments for FY2022-FY2026. Observers used the term Pacific Deterrence Initiative (PDI) or Indo-Pacific Deterrence Initiative (IPDI)—a Pacific or Indo-Pacific analog to the European Deterrence Initiative (EDI) discussed in the next section—to refer to proposals for making various investments for strengthening U.S. and allied military capabilities in the Pacific region.

Section 1251 of the FY2021 National Defense Authorization Act (H.R. 6395/P.L. 116-283 of January 1, 2021) directed DOD to establish a Pacific Deterrence Initiative "to carry out prioritized activities to enhance the United States deterrence and defense posture in the Indo-Pacific region, assure allies and partners, and increase capability and readiness in the Indo-Pacific region." The provision authorized $2.235 billion to carry out the initiative in FY2021; directed DOD to submit a report not later than February 15, 2021, on future-year activities and resources for the initiative; directed DOD's annual budget submissions, starting with the submission for FY2022, to include a detailed

(continued...)

As noted earlier, given finite U.S. defense resources, strengthening U.S. military force deployments in the Indo-Pacific region could involve reducing U.S. force deployments to other locations.

U.S. and NATO Capabilities in Europe

The emergence of intensified competition with Russia—which was made more observable by Russia's seizure and announced annexation of Ukraine in March 2014 (which the United States does not recognize)[80] and Russia's subsequent actions in eastern Ukraine, and then further underscored by Russia's invasion of multiple parts of Ukraine starting on February 24, 2022—has led to a renewed focus in U.S. defense planning on strengthening U.S. and NATO military capabilities for countering potential Russian aggression in Europe.[81] Some observers have expressed particular concern about the ability of the United States and its NATO allies to defend the Baltic members of NATO in the event of a fast-paced Russian military move into one or more of those countries. The Biden Administration's October 2022 NDS states

> *Europe.* The Department will maintain its bedrock commitment to NATO collective security, working alongside Allies and partners to deter, defend, and build resilience against further Russian military aggression and acute forms of gray zone coercion. As we continue contributing to NATO capabilities and readiness—including through improvements to our posture in Europe and our extended nuclear deterrence commitments—the Department will work with Allies bilaterally and through NATO's established processes to better focus NATO capability development and military modernization to address Russia's military threat. The approach will emphasize ready, interoperable combat power in contested environments across NATO forces, particularly air forces and other joint precision strike capabilities, and critical enablers such as intelligence, surveillance, and reconnaissance (ISR) and electronic warfare platforms. The Department will collaborate with Allies and partners to build capacity along Europe's eastern flank, strengthening defensive anti-area/access-denial capabilities and indications and warning; expanding readiness, training, and exercises; and promoting resilience, including against hybrid and cyber actions.[82]

The United States has taken a number of steps to strengthen the U.S. military presence and U.S. military operations in and around Europe. In mainland Europe, these actions have included steps to reinforce Army and Air Force capabilities and operations in central Europe, including actions to increase the U.S. military presence in countries such as Poland.[83] In northern Europe, U.S. actions have included presence operations and exercises by the Marine Corps in Norway and by

---

budget display for the initiative; and directed DOD to brief Congress not later than March 1, 2021, and annually thereafter, on the budget proposal and programs for the initiative. Section 1251 of P.L. 116-283 also repealed Section 1251 of the FY2018 National Defense Authorization Act (H.R. 2810/P.L. 115-91 of December 12, 2017), as most recently amended by Section 12534 of the FY2019 National Defense Authorization Act (H.R. 5515/P.L. 115-232 of August 13, 2018). Section 1251 of P.L. 115-91 directed DOD to establish an Indo-Asia-Pacific Stability Initiative, and Section 1253 of P.L. 115-232 modified the initiative's name to Indo-Pacific Stability Initiative and made other changes to the initiative.

[80] The State Department states that "the United States does not, and will never, recognize Russia's purported annexation of Crimea." (State Department, "Crimea Is Ukraine," press statement, Antony J. Blinken, Secretary of State, February 25, 2021.)

[81] See, for example, CRS In Focus IF11130, *United States European Command: Overview and Key Issues*, by Kathleen J. McInnis, Brendan W. McGarry, and Paul Belkin.

[82] Department of Defense, *2022 National Defense Strategy of the United States of America*, cover letter dated October 27, 2022, p. 15.

[83] See, for example, CRS In Focus IF11280, *U.S. Military Presence in Poland*, by Andrew Feickert, Kathleen J. McInnis, and Derek E. Mix.

---

the U.S. Navy in northern European waters. In southern Europe, the Mediterranean has re-emerged as an operating area of importance for the Navy. Some of these actions, particularly for mainland Europe, are assembled into an annually funded package within the overall DOD budget originally called the European Reassurance Initiative and now called the European Deterrence Initiative (EDI).[84] In response to Russia's invasion of multiple parts of Ukraine starting on February 24, 2022, the United States has deployed additional Army and Air Force units to locations in NATO allied countries in Europe.

Renewed concern over NATO capabilities for deterring potential Russian aggression in Europe has been a key factor in U.S. actions intended to encourage the NATO allies to increase their own defense spending levels. NATO leaders since 2014 have announced a series of initiatives for increasing their defense spending and refocusing NATO away from "out of area" (i.e., beyond-Europe) operations, and back toward a focus on territorial defense and deterrence in Europe itself.[85] Following Russia's invasion of multiple parts of Ukraine starting on February 24, 2022, some NATO allies have announced steps to increase their defense budgets or otherwise bolster their military capabilities.

New Operational Concepts

The emergence of GPC has led to a focus by U.S. military services on the development of new operational concepts—that is, new ways of employing U.S. military forces—particularly for countering improving Chinese anti-access/area-denial (A2/AD) forces[86] in the Indo-Pacific region. These new operational concepts include Multi-Domain Operations (MDO) for the Army and Air Force, Agile Combat Employment for the Air Force, Distributed Maritime Operations (DMO) for the Navy and Marine Corps, and Expeditionary Advanced Base Operations (EABO) for the Marine Corps.[87] In general, these new operational concepts are more distributed and networked, make greater use of unmanned vehicles, and employ a higher degree of integration between operating domains (i.e., space, cyberspace, air, land, sea, and undersea). In February 2023, the Joint Chiefs of Staff released a new joint concept for competing.[88]

Capabilities for High-End Conventional Warfare

The emergence of GPC has led to a renewed emphasis in U.S. defense planning on capabilities for conducting so-called high-end conventional warfare, meaning large-scale, high-intensity, technologically sophisticated conventional warfare against adversaries with similarly

---

[84] For further discussion, see CRS In Focus IF10946, *The European Deterrence Initiative: A Budgetary Overview*, by Paul Belkin and Hibbah Kaileh.

[85] For additional discussion, see CRS Report R45652, *Assessing NATO's Value*, by Paul Belkin. See also CRS Report R46066, *NATO: Key Issues for the 117th Congress*, by Paul Belkin.

[86] The term *anti-access/area-denial (A2/AD) forces* generally refers to military forces that are intended to keep opposing military forces from entering and operating within certain areas or regions, particularly areas or regions that are inside or adjacent to the homeland of the country deploying the A2/AD forces. In discussions of naval forces, such forces in the past have been referred to as sea-denial forces.

[87] For more on EABO and DMO, see CRS Report RL32665, *Navy Force Structure and Shipbuilding Plans: Background and Issues for Congress*, by Ronald O'Rourke.

[88] Joint Chiefs of Staff, *Joint Concept for Competing*, February 10, 2023, 75 pp. Some observers have argued that DOD should be able to modify its planning rapidly to adapt to evolving international security requirements. See Joe Gould, "Is Pentagon Planning up to the Job for Great Power Competition?" *Military Times*, February 17, 2023, which discusses Peter C. Combe II, Benjamin Jensen, and Adrian Bogart, "Rethinking Risk in Great Power Competition," Center for Strategic and International Studies (CSIS), February 17, 2023.

---

sophisticated military capabilities.[89] Capabilities for high-end conventional warfare can differ, sometimes significantly, from capabilities required or optimized for the kinds of counterterrorism or counter-insurgency operations that were more at the center of U.S. defense planning and operations following the terrorist attacks of September 11, 2001. Many current DOD acquisition programs, exercises, and warfighting experiments have been initiated, accelerated, increased in scope, given higher priority, or had their continuation justified as a consequence of the renewed U.S. emphasis on high-end conventional warfare.

Weapon acquisition programs that can be linked to preparing for high-end warfare include (to mention only a few examples) those for procuring advanced aircraft such as the F-35 Joint Strike Fighter (JSF)[90] and the next-generation B-21 long-range bomber,[91] highly capable warships such as the Virginia-class attack submarine[92] and DDG-51 class Aegis destroyer,[93] ballistic missile defense (BMD) capabilities,[94] longer-ranged land-attack and anti-ship weapons,[95] new types of weapons such as lasers,[96] new C4ISR (command, control, communications, computers, intelligence, surveillance, and reconnaissance) capabilities,[97] military space capabilities,[98] electronic warfare capabilities,[99] military cyber capabilities,[100] hypersonic weapons,[101] and the

---

[89] See, for example, Connie Lee, "ASC NEWS: U.S. Military Re-Emphasizing Large Warfighting Exercises (UPDATED)," *National Defense*, September 14, 2020. See also Christopher Layne, "Coming Storms, The Return of Great-Power War," *Foreign Affairs*, November/December 2020.

[90] See CRS Report RL30563, *F-35 Joint Strike Fighter (JSF) Program*, by John R. Hoehn.

[91] See CRS Report R44463, *Air Force B-21 Raider Long-Range Strike Bomber*, coordinated by John R. Hoehn.

[92] See CRS Report RL32418, *Navy Virginia-Class Submarine Program and AUKUS Submarine Proposal: Background and Issues for Congress*, by Ronald O'Rourke.

[93] See CRS Report RL32109, *Navy DDG-51 and DDG-1000 Destroyer Programs: Background and Issues for Congress*, by Ronald O'Rourke.

[94] See CRS In Focus IF10541, *Defense Primer: Ballistic Missile Defense*, coordinated by Kelley M. Sayler; CRS In Focus IF11623, *Hypersonic Missile Defense: Issues for Congress*, by Kelley M. Sayler ; and CRS Report RL33745, *Navy Aegis Ballistic Missile Defense (BMD) Program: Background and Issues for Congress*, by Ronald O'Rourke.

[95] See CRS In Focus IF11353, *Defense Primer: U.S. Precision-Guided Munitions*, coordinated by Nathan J. Lucas.

[96] See CRS In Focus IF11882, *Defense Primer: Directed-Energy Weapons*, by Kelley M. Sayler; CRS Report R46925, *Department of Defense Directed Energy Weapons: Background and Issues for Congress*, coordinated by Kelley M. Sayler; CRS Report R45098, *U.S. Army Weapons-Related Directed Energy (DE) Programs: Background and Potential Issues for Congress*, by Andrew Feickert; and CRS Report R44175, *Navy Shipboard Lasers: Background and Issues for Congress*, by Ronald O'Rourke.

[97] CRS In Focus IF11493, *Joint All-Domain Command and Control (JADC2)*, by John R. Hoehn; CRS Report R46725, *Joint All-Domain Command and Control: Background and Issues for Congress*, by John R. Hoehn; and CRS In Focus IF11866, *Advanced Battle Management System (ABMS)*, by John R. Hoehn. See also Rebecca K.C. Hersman and Reja Younis, *The Adversary Gets a Vote, Advanced Situational Awsareness and Implications for Integrated Deterrence in an Era of Great Power Competition*, CSIS, September 2021 (posted online September 27, 2021), 10 pp.

[98] See CRS In Focus IF11895, *Space as a Warfighting Domain: Issues for Congress*, by Stephen M. McCall; CRS In Focus IF10337, *Challenges to the United States in Space*, by Stephen M. McCall; CRS In Focus IF11531, *Defense Primer: National Security Space Launch*, coordinated by Kelley M. Sayler; and CRS Report R46211, *National Security Space Launch*, by Stephen M. McCall.

[99] See CRS In Focus IF11118, *Defense Primer: Electronic Warfare*, by John R. Hoehn; and CRS Insight IN11705, *FY2022 Electronic Warfare Funding Trends*, by John R. Hoehn.

[100] See CRS In Focus IF11995, *Use of Force in Cyberspace*, by Catherine A. Theohary; CRS In Focus IF10537, *Defense Primer: Cyberspace Operations*, by Catherine A. Theohary; and CRS In Focus IF11292, *Convergence of Cyberspace Operations and Electronic Warfare*, by Catherine A. Theohary and John R. Hoehn.

[101] See CRS In Focus IF11459, *Defense Primer: Hypersonic Boost-Glide Weapons*, by Kelley M. Sayler ; CRS Report R45811, *Hypersonic Weapons: Background and Issues for Congress*, by Kelley M. Sayler; and CRS In Focus IF11991, *The U.S. Army's Long-Range Hypersonic Weapon (LRHW)*, by Andrew Feickert.

military uses of robotics and autonomous unmanned vehicles, quantum technology, and artificial intelligence (AI).[102]

Preparing for high-end conventional warfare could also involve making changes in U.S. military training and exercises[103] and reorienting the missions and training of U.S. special operations forces.[104] On February 8, 2023, the Intelligence and Special Operations subcommittee of the House Armed Services Committee held a hearing on the role of special operations forces in great power competition. On May 17, 2023, the Emerging Threats and Capabilities subcommittee of the Senate Armed Services Committee held a hearing on the role of special operations forces in supporting the national defense strategy, including activities that contribute to long-term strategic competition with China and Russia.

Maintaining U.S. Superiority in Conventional Weapon Technologies

As part of the renewed emphasis on capabilities for high-end conventional warfare, DOD officials have expressed concern that U.S. superiority in conventional weapon technologies has narrowed or in some cases been eliminated by China and (in certain areas) Russia. In response, DOD has taken a number of actions that are intended to help maintain or regain U.S. superiority in conventional weapon technologies, including increased research and development funding for new militarily applicable technologies such as artificial intelligence (AI), autonomous unmanned weapons, hypersonic weapons, directed-energy weapons, biotechnology, and quantum technology.[105] Controls on exports to China, Russia, and other countries of advanced technologies

---

[102] See CRS In Focus IF11105, *Defense Primer: Emerging Technologies*, by Kelley M. Sayler; CRS Report R46458, *Emerging Military Technologies: Background and Issues for Congress*, by Kelley M. Sayler; CRS In Focus IF11150, *Defense Primer: U.S. Policy on Lethal Autonomous Weapon Systems*, by Kelley M. Sayler; CRS Report R46458, *Emerging Military Technologies: Background and Issues for Congress*, by Kelley M. Sayler; CRS In Focus IF11836, *Defense Primer: Quantum Technology*, by Kelley M. Sayler; and CRS Report R45178, *Artificial Intelligence and National Security*, by Kelley M. Sayler.

[103] See, for example, Tom Greenwood and Owen Daniels, "The Pentagon Should Train for—and Not Just Talk About—Great-Power Competition," *War on the Rocks*, May 8, 2020.

[104] See, for example, Drew F. Lawrence, "Defending a Mock Invasion of Taiwan Signals Shift for Army Special Operations After Years of Counterinsurgency," *Military.com*, April 29, 2023; Bryan P. Fenton, "How Special Operations Forces Must Meet the Challenges of a New Era," *Defense One*, May 11, 2023; Lee Ferran, "The 'Morale Challenge' Facing Some Special Operators in the Era of Great Power Competition," *Breaking Defense*, May 11, 2023; Todd South, "Special Operations Role in Great Power Competition Needs Work," *Military Times*, May 11, 2023; Sam Skove, "With Lessons from Ukraine, US Special Forces Reinvents Itself for a Fight with China," *Defense One*, May 1, 2023; Drew F. Lawrence, "Defending a Mock Invasion of Taiwan Signals Shift for Army Special Operations After Years of Counterinsurgency," *Military.com*, April 29, 2023; David Ucko, "Indispensable but Insufficient: The Role and Limits of Special Operations in Strategic Competition," *Lawfare*, February 19, 2023; Spencer Reed, "Recalibrating Special Operations Risk Tolerance for the Future Fight," *War on the Rocks*, January 31, 2023; Elizabeth Howe, "Special Operators Lack 'Seat at the Table' in Post-Counterterror Pentagon, SOF Leaders Say," *Defense One*, November 18, 2022; Stavros Atlamazoglou, "US Special Operators Are Picking Up a Softer Skill as They Refocus on Countering China," *Business Insider*, June 28, 2022; Tom Hammerle and Mike Pultusker, "Special Operations Are Deterrence Operations: How United States Special Operations Forces Should Be Used in Strategic Competition," *Small Wars Journal*, May 24, 2022; Stew Magnuson, "Special Ops Tech Pivots to Indo-Pacific Challenges," *National Defense*, May 20, 2022; Stephen Watts et al., *Countering Russia, The Role of Special Operations Forces in Strategic Competition*, RAND, 2021, 95 pp.

For more on U.S. special operations forces, see CRS In Focus IF10545, *Defense Primer: Special Operations Forces*, by Barbara Salazar Torreon and Andrew Feickert; and CRS Report RS21048, *U.S. Special Operations Forces (SOF): Background and Issues for Congress*, by Andrew Feickert.

[105] See the CRS reports cited in footnote 101 and footnote 102.

---

with potential military uses form another part of this effort.[106] The Biden Administration's October 2022 NDS states

> *Make the Right Technology Investments*. The United States' technological edge has long been a foundation of our military advantage. The Department will support the innovation ecosystem, both at home and in expanded partnerships with our Allies and partners. We will fuel research and development for advanced capabilities, including in directed energy, hypersonics, integrated sensing, and cyber. We will seed opportunities in biotechnology, quantum science, advanced materials, and clean-energy technology. We will be a fast-follower where market forces are driving commercialization of militarily-relevant capabilities in trusted artificial intelligence and autonomy, integrated network system-of-systems, microelectronics, space, renewable energy generation and storage, and human-machine interfaces. Because Joint Force operations increasingly rely on data-driven technologies and integration of diverse data sources, the Department will implement institutional reforms that integrate our data, software, and artificial intelligence efforts and speed their delivery to the warfighter.[107]

A February 2, 2022, press report stated

> The Pentagon's research and engineering chief is crafting a new strategy for investment in 14 critical technology areas, writing in a new memo that "creative application" of emerging concepts is key to maintaining an edge over adversaries.

> The Feb. 1 memo, first reported by *Inside Defense*, does not lay out a timeline for when the strategy will be complete, but notes the work will be informed by the 2022 National Defense Strategy and structured around three pillars: Mission focus, foundation building and succeeding through teamwork.

> "Successful competition requires imagining our military capability as an ever-evolving collective, not a static inventory of weapons in development or sustainment," Undersecretary of Defense for Research and Engineering Heidi Shyu wrote in the memo, obtained by C4ISRNET. "In many cases, effective competition benefits from sidestepping symmetric arms races and instead comes from the creative application of new concepts with emerging science and technology."

> The technologies identified in the memo ranges from "seed areas"—like quantum science, biotechnology, advanced materials and future-generation wireless technology—to commercially available capabilities such as artificial intelligence, space, microelectronics, integrated networks, renewable energy, human-machine interfaces and advanced computing and software.

> The memo also highlights technology needs that are specific to the Defense Department, including hypersonic weapons, directed energy, cyber and integrated sensing.

> "By focusing efforts and investments into these 14 critical technology areas, the department will accelerate transitioning key capabilities to the military services and combatant commands," Shyu writes. "As the department's strategy evolves and technologies change, the department will update its critical technology priorities."[108]

---

[106] For additional discussion, see CRS In Focus IF11627, *U.S. Export Controls and China*, by Karen M. Sutter and Christopher A. Casey; CRS In Focus IF11154, *Export Controls: Key Challenges*, by Christopher A. Casey ; CRS Report R46814, *The U.S. Export Control System and the Export Control Reform Act of 2018*, by Paul K. Kerr and Christopher A. Casey. See also John Schaus and Elizabeth Hoffman, "Is ITAR Working in an Era of Great Power Competition?" Center for Strategic and International Studies (CSIS), February 24, 2023.

[107] Department of Defense, *2022 National Defense Strategy of the United States of America*, cover letter dated October 27, 2022, p. 19.

[108] Courtney Albon, "New Strategy Will Harness Emerging Tech to Beat Adversaries," *Defense News*, February 2, 2022. See also the CRS reports cited in footnote 102.

Innovation and Speed of U.S. Weapon System Development and Deployment

In addition to the above-mentioned efforts for maintaining U.S. superiority in conventional weapon technologies, DOD is placing new emphasis on innovation and speed in weapon system development and deployment, so as to more quickly and effectively transition new weapon technologies into fielded systems.[109] The Biden Administration's October 2022 NDS states

> *Transform the Foundation of the Future Force.* Building the Joint Force [i.e., U.S. military] called for by this strategy requires overhauling the Department's force development, design, and business management practices. Our current system is too slow and too focused on acquiring systems not designed to address the most critical challenges we now face. This orientation leaves little incentive to design open systems that can rapidly incorporate cutting-edge technologies, creating longer-term challenges with obsolescence, interoperability, and cost effectiveness. The Department will instead reward rapid experimentation, acquisition, and fielding. We will better align requirements, resourcing, and acquisition, and undertake a campaign of learning to identify the most promising concepts, incorporating emerging technologies in the commercial and military sectors for solving our key operational challenges. We will design transition pathways to divest from systems that are less relevant to advancing the force planning guidance, and partner to equip the defense industrial base to support more relevant modernization efforts.[110]

The individual military services have taken various actions to increase innovation and speed in their weapon acquisition programs. Some of these actions make use of special acquisition authorities provided by Congress that are intended in part to reduce the time needed to transition new weapon technologies into fielded systems, including Other Transaction Authority (OTA) and what is known as Section 804 Middle Tier authority.[111]

On January 23, 2020, DOD released a new defense acquisition framework, called the Adaptive Acquisition Framework, that is intended to substantially accelerate the DOD's process for developing and fielding new weapons.[112] In previewing the new framework in October 2019, DOD described it as "the most transformational acquisition policy change we've seen in decades."[113]

---

[109] See, for example, Briana Reilly, "With Rapid Experimentation Effort, DOD Looks to Build Up Tech Transition Pathways," *Inside Defense*, April 13, 2022; Matthew Beinart, "Hicks Says RDER Will Help Address DoD's 'Complicated System' for Advancing Promising Tech," *Defense Daily*, April 12, 2022.

[110] Department of Defense, *2022 National Defense Strategy of the United States of America*, cover letter dated October 27, 2022, p. 19.

[111] See, for example, CRS Report R45521, *Department of Defense Use of Other Transaction Authority: Background, Analysis, and Issues for Congress*, by Heidi M. Peters; Government Accountability Office, *Defense Acquisitions[:] DOD's Use of Other Transactions for Prototype Projects Has Increased*, GAO-20-84, November 2019, 31 pp.; Matt Donovan and Will Roper, "Section 804 Gives the US an Advantage in Great Power Competition with China and Russia," *Defense News*, August 7, 2019; Justin Doubleday, "Section 809 Panel Chair Warns Against 'Abuse' of Other Transaction Agreements," Inside Defense, October 3, 2019; Aaron Greg, "Seeking an Edge over Geopolitical Rivals, Pentagon Exploits an Obscure Regulatory Workaround," *Washington Post*, October 18, 2019; Scott Maucione, "Special Report: Failure Is an Option for DoD's Experimental Agency, But How Much?" *Federal News Network*, October 30, 2019; Colin Clark, "OTA Prototyping Nearly Triples To $3.7B: GAO," *Breaking Defense*, November 26, 2019; Eric Lofgren, "Too Many Cooks in the DoD: New Policy May Suppress Rapid Acquisition," *Defense News*, January 2, 2020.

[112] See, for example, Tony Bertuca, "Pentagon releases New Guidelines to Accelerate Acquisition," *Inside Defense*, January 24, 2020. The operation of the framework is set forth in DOD Instruction (DODI) 5000.02, *Operation of the Adaptive Acquisition Framework*, January 23, 2020, 17 pp.

[113] See, for example, Tony Bertuca, "[Ellen] Lord: Pentagon Is 'On the Brink' of Acquisition Transformation," *Inside Defense*, October 18, 2019. See also Richard Sisk, "Pentagon Debuts Yet Another Plan to Speed Up Weapons Buys," *Military.com*, October 8, 2020.

AI-32

Some observers argue that DOD is not doing enough or moving quickly enough to generate and implement innovations in response to GPC, and have proposed steps for doing more or moving more quickly.[114] A January 2020 GAO report on weapon system reliability in defense acquisition, however, states

> DOD has taken steps to accelerate weapon system development, and decision-making authority has been delegated to the military services. In an environment emphasizing speed, without senior leadership focus on a broader range of key reliability practices, DOD runs the risk of delivering less reliable systems than promised to the warfighter and spending more than anticipated on rework and maintenance of major weapon systems.[115]

DOD officials and other observers argue that to facilitate greater innovation and speed in weapon system development and deployment, U.S. defense acquisition policy and the oversight paradigm for assessing the success of acquisition programs will need to be adjusted to place a greater emphasis on innovation and speed as measures of merit in defense acquisition policy, alongside more traditional measures of merit such as minimizing cost growth, schedule delays, and problems in testing. As a consequence, they argue, defense acquisition policy and the oversight paradigm for assessing the success of acquisition programs should place more emphasis on time as a risk factor and feature more experimentation, risk-taking, and tolerance of failure during development, with a lack of failures in testing potentially being viewed in some cases not as an indication of success, but of inadequate innovation or speed of development.[116]

---

[114] See, for example, Charles Beames, "In Race with China, Pentagon Must Prioritize Speed in Acquisition," *Breaking Defense*, July 19, 2023; Mark Esper and Deborah Lee James, "To Deter Conflict, the Pentagon Must Accelerate Innovation Adoption," *The Hill*, March 9, 2023; Thomas G. Mahnken, Evan B. Montgomery, and Tyler Hacker, *Innovating for Great Power Competition An Examination of Service and Joint Innovation Efforts*, Center for Strategic and Budgetary Assessments, 2023, 82 pp.; Lauren C. Williams, "Is the Pentagon Changing Fast Enough?" *Defense One*, November 14, 2023; Jules Hurst, "Fixing Defense Innovation: Rewriting Acquisition and Security Regulations," *War on the Rocks*, October 7, 2022; Melissa Flagg, "No Time to Waste: The Pentagon Needs an Innovation Overhaul, A Technological Transition Will Take Time, but the United States Cannot Fight and Win in This New Multipolar World Unless It Begins Today," *National Interest*, August 21, 2022; Thomas Newdick, "China Acquiring New Weapons Five Times Faster Than U.S. Warns Top Official," *The Drive*, July 6, 2022; Dan Ward and Matt MacGregor, *Arming the Eagle, Outpacing the Dragon: Understanding and Out Competing China's Defense Acquisition And Innovation*, Mitre Corporation, June 2022, 29 pp.; Elaine McCusker and Emily Coletta, "Is the U.S. Military Ready to Defend Taiwan?" *National Interest*, February 6, 2022; Christopher Zember, "Change How OTAs Are Used to Make Them an Essential Tool Against China," *Breaking Defense*, February 3, 2022; Robert A. McDonald Sr., M. Sam Araki, and Robert Wilkie, "These Seven Principles Could Help DoD Acquisition in the Face of the China Threat," *Defense News*, February 1, 2022; Daniel K. Lim, "Startups and the Defense Department's Compliance Labyrinth," *War on the Rocks*, January 3, 2022.

[115] Government Accountability Office, *Defense Acquisitions[:] Senior Leaders Should Emphasize Key Practices to Improve Weapon System Reliability*, GAO-20-151, January 2020, summary page.

[116] See, for example, Joel Gehrke, "China's Military Planners Move Faster Than Pentagon Bureaucrats, Official Says," *Washington Examiner*, May 3, 2022; Sean Carberry, "Air Force Must Embrace Risk to Counter China," *National Defense*, May 2, 2022; Tate Nurkin, "To Catch China and Russia in Hypersonic Race, US Must Embrace Risk Now," *Breaking Defense*, February 9, 2022; Corey Dickstein, "Vice Chairman Nominee Says US Military Must Adapt New Tech Faster to Compete with China, Russia," *Stars and Stripes*, December 8, 2021; Sam LaGrone, "Eliminating 'Risk Aversion' Key to Weapons Development, Says Vice Chair Nominee Grady," *USNI News*, December 8, 2021; Bryan Clark, "Pentagon And Congress Risk Bungling Drive To Modernize U.S. Military," *Forbes*, July 8, 2020; John Grady, "Officials: U.S. Must Move Faster in Testing and Fielding Hypersonics, 5G Networks," *USNI News*, June 30, 2020; Michèle A. Flournoy and Gabrielle Chefitz, "Breaking the Logjam: How the Pentagon Can Build Trust with Congress," *Defense News*, April 1, 2020; Ankit Panda, "Getting Critical Technologies Into Defense Applications," *National Interest*, February 1, 2020; Ankit Panda, "Critical Technologies and Great Power Competition," *Diplomat*, January 29, 2020; Michael Rubin, "The Simple Reason Why America Could Lose the Next Cold War to Russia or China," *National Interest*, January 14, 2020; George Franz and Scott Bachand, "China and Russia Beware: How the Pentagon Can Win the Tech Arms Race," *National Interest*, November 29, 2019; Scott Maucione, "Special Report: Failure Is an Option for DoD's Experimental Agency, But How Much?" *Federal News Week*, October 30, 2019; (continued...)

Mobilization Capabilities for Extended-Length Conflict

The emergence of GPC has led to an increased emphasis in discussions of U.S. defense on U.S. mobilization capabilities for an extended-length conflict.[117] The term *mobilization* is often used to refer specifically to preparations for activating U.S. military reserve force personnel and inducting additional people into the Armed Forces. In this report, it is used more broadly, to refer to various activities, including those relating to the ability of the industrial base to support U.S. military operations in a larger-scale, extended-length conflict against China or Russia. Under this broader definition, mobilization capabilities include but are not limited to capabilities for

- inducting and training additional military personnel to expand the size of the force or replace personnel who are killed or wounded;

- producing new weapons and supplies to replace those expended in the earlier stages of a conflict, and delivering those weapons and supplies to distantly deployed U.S. forces in a timely manner;

- repairing battle damage to ships, aircraft, and vehicles;

- replacing satellites or other support assets that are lost in combat; and

- manufacturing spare parts and consumable items.

Some observers have expressed concern about the adequacy of U.S. mobilization capabilities, particularly since this was not a major defense-planning concern during the 20 to 25 years of the post–Cold War era, and have recommended various actions to improve those capabilities.[118]

Sydney J. Freedberg Jr., "Stop Wasting Time So We Can Beat China: DoD R&D Boss, Griffin," *Breaking Defense*, August 9, 2018.

[117] See, for example, Raphael S. Cohen, "The U.S. Should Get Over Its Short War Obsession," *Foreign Policy*, March 28, 2023.

Hal Brands, "Win or Lose, U.S. War Against China or Russia Won't Be Short," *Bloomberg*, June 14, 2021.

[118] See, for example, Andrew A. Michta, "Pivot to the Pacific? That Misses the Point, We Need a Rebuilt Defense Industrial Base to Make Our Forces Ready for Combat in Any Theater," *Wall Street Journal*, June 23, 2023; Cynthia Cook, "Reviving the Arsenal of Democracy: Steps for Surging Defense Industrial Capacity," Center for Strategic and International Studies (CSIS), March 14, 2023; Aaron Friedberg and Michael Wessel, "With China, America Faces a Preparedness Crisis," *The Hill*, January 6, 2023; Maiya Clark, "Revitalizing the National Defense Stockpile for an Era of Great-Power Competition," Heritage Foundation, January 4, 2022; Elbridge A. Colby and Alexander B. Gray, "America's Industrial Base Isn't Ready for War with China, Washington Must Invest Immediately in a Domestic Capacity to Build and Repair Military Hardware," *Wall Street Journal*, August 18, 2022; Hal Brands and Michael Beckley, "Washington Is Preparing for the Wrong War With China, A Conflict Would Be Long and Messy," *Foreign Affairs*, December 16, 2021; Seth Cropsey and Harry Halem, "The U.S. Is Wholly Unequipped to Resupply Forces in a Great-Power Conflict," *Defense News*, October 21, 2021; Marcus Weisgerber, "Digital Engineering Could Speed Wartime Arms Production," *Defense One*, June 8, 2021; Government Accountability Office, *Navy Ships[:] Timely Actions Needed to Improve Planning and Develop Capabilities for Battle Damage Repair*, GAO-21-246, June 2021, 46 pp.; Tristan Abbey, "America's Stockpiles Are Hardly Strategic," *Defense One*, February 9, 2021; Mark Cancian and Adam Saxton, "US War Surge Production Too Slow, CSIS Finds," *Breaking Defense*, January 19, 2021; Robert "Jake" Bebber, "State of War, State of Mind: Reconsidering Mobilization in the Information Age, Pt. 1," Center for International Maritime Security, January 11, 2021 (drawn from Robert "Jake" Bebber, "State of War, State of Mind: Reconsidering Mobilization in the Information Age," *Journal of Political Risk*, October 20, 2020); Mark F. Cancian, Adam Saxton, Owen Helman, Lee Ann Bryan, and Nidal Morrison, *Industrial Mobilization: Assessing Surge Capabilities, Wartime Risk, and System Brittleness*, CSIS, January 2021, 57 pp.; Ryan Pickrell, "China Is the World's Biggest Shipbuilder, and Its Ability to Rapidly Produce New Warships Would Be a 'Huge advantage' in a Long Fight with the US, Experts Say," *Business Insider*, September 8, 2020; Marcus Weisgerber, "US Shipyards Lack Needed Repair Capacity, Admiral Says," *Defense One*, August 27, 2020; Megan Eckstein, "Lack of U.S. Warship Repair Capacity Worrying Navy," *USNI News*, August 26, 2020; Paul McLeary, "Navy Plans For Wartime Ship Surge; Looks To Small Commercial Yards," *Breaking Defense*, August 25, 2020; Patrick Savage, What If It Doesn't End Quickly? Reconsidering US Preparedness for Protracted Conventional War," Modern War Institute, July 23, 2020; Elsa B. Kania (continued...)

Concerns over U.S. industrial mobilization capabilities have been reinforced by the U.S. and allied response to Russia's invasion of multiple parts of Ukraine starting on February 24, 2022, which has spotlighted

- how rapidly certain weapons (particularly precision-guided munitions) can be expended in modern warfare;

- the finite U.S. and allied inventories of precision-guided munitions, air-defense systems, and other equipment; and

- limits on existing U.S. and allied industrial capacity for producing new weapons and equipment to replace those transferred to Ukraine and to increase the size of U.S. and allied inventories to levels higher than those that were planned prior to Russia's invasion.[119]

and Emma Moore, "The US Is Unprepared to Mobilize for Great Power Conflict," *Defense One*, July 21, 2019; Alan L. Gropman, "America Needs to Prepare for a Great Power War," *National Interest*, February 7, 2018; Joseph Whitlock, "The Army's Mobilization Problem," U.S. Army War College War Room, October 13, 2017; Mark Cancian, "Long Wars and Industrial Mobilization," *War on the Rocks*, August 8, 2017; David Barno and Nora Bensahel, "Mirages of War: Six Illusions from Our Recent Conflicts," *War on the Rocks*, April 11, 2017; Robert Haddick, "Competitive Mobilization: How Would We Fare Against China?" *War on the Rocks*, March 15, 2016; David Barno and Nora Bensahel, "Preparing for the Next Big War," *War on the Rocks*, January 26, 2016. See also William Greenwalt, *Leveraging the National Technology Industrial Base to Address Great-Power Competition: The Imperative to Integrate Industrial Capabilities of Close Allies*, Atlantic Council, April 2019, 58 pp.

[119] See, for example, Tyler Hacker, *Beyond Precision: Maintaining America's Strike Advantage in Great Power Conflict*, Center for Strategic and Budgetary Assessments (CSBA), 2023 (posted online June 12, 2023), 134 pp.; Vasabjit Banerjee and Benjamin Tkach, "Munitions Return to a Place of Prominence in National Security," *War on the Rocks*, March 16, 2023; Paul McLeary and Alexander Ward, "New Pentagon Office Looks to Speed Up Weapons Buys," *Politico Pro*, March 15, 2023; Marcus Weisgerber, "Pentagon Creates Cell to Oversee Expansion of Weapon Production Lines," *Defense One*, March 15, 2023; Marcus Weisgerber, "Memo Details Effort to Boost Production of Weapons Sent to Ukraine," *Defense One*, February 8, 2023; Caroline Coudriet, "Lawmakers Worry About Weapons-Makers' Ability to Meet Demand," *CQ*, February 6, 2023; Seth G. Jones, "Empty Bins in a Wartime Environment: The Challenge to the U.S. Defense Industrial Base," Center for Strategic and International Studies (CSIS), January 23, 2023; Gordon Lubold, "U.S. Weapons Industry Unprepared for a China Conflict, Report Says," *Wall Street Journal*, January 23, 2023; Tony Bertuca, "Ukraine conflict sharpens industrial policy debate among top U.S. defense players," *Inside Defense*, January 5, 2023; Chris Laudati, "The Precarious State of U.S. Defense Stockpiles," *National Defense*, November 18, 2022; Eric Lofgren, "Precision Guided Munitions Production Is Totally Inadequate," *Acquisition Talk*, November 22, 2022; Mike Stone, "Pentagon, U.S. Arms Makers to Talk Russia, Labor and Supply Chain," *Reuters*, November 4, 2022; Thomas G. Mahnken, "Could America Win a New World War? What It Would Take to Defeat Both China and Russia," *Foreign Affairs*, October 27, 2022; John Ferrari, "Four Steps the Pentagon Can Take to Fix the Munitions Industrial Base," *The Hill*, October 17, 2022; Bradley Bowman and Mark Montgomery, "America's Arsenal Is in Need of Life Support," *Defense News*, October 12, 2022; John Ferrari, "Cannibalizing the Arsenal of Democracy in Turbulent Times," *Military Times*, October 12, 2022; John Ismay and Lara Jakes, "Meeting in Brussels Signifies a Turning Point for Allies Arming Ukraine, Defense Officials Responsible for Purchasing Weapons for More Than 40 Nations Discussed How to Ramp Up Production for a Potentially Yearslong War," *New York Times*, September 28, 2022; Andrew White, "Ukraine Shows Need for NATO 'Magazine Depth': Raytheon Exec," *Breaking Defense*, July 20, 2022; David Johnson, "A Modern-Day Frederick The Great? The End of Short, Sharp Wars," *War on the Rocks*, July 5, 2022; Daniel Michaels, "Lessons of Russia's War in Ukraine: You Can't Hide and Weapons Stockpiles Are Essential," *Wall Street Journal*, July 4, 2022; Alex Vershinin, "The Return of Industrial Warfare," RUSI, June 17, 2022; Trae Stephens, "Rebooting the Arsenal of Democracy," *War on the Rocks*, June 6, 2022; Conrad Crane, "Too Fragile to Fight: Could the U.S. Military Withstand a War of Attrition?," *War on the Rocks*, May 9, 2022; "Because of Ukraine, America's Arsenal of Democracy Is Depleting, The War Raises Worries about America's Ability to Arm Its Friends," *Economist*, May 7, 2022; Bill Greenwalt and Dustin Walker, "How Biden's 'Buy American' Is Undermining the Arsenal of Democracy," *Breaking Defense*, May 3, 2022; Thomas G. Mahnken, "The US Needs a New Approach to Producing Weapons. Just Look at Ukraine," *Defense News*, April 26, 2022.

AI-35

On April 24, 2019, the National Commission on Military, National, and Public Service, a commission created by the FY2017 National Defense Authorization Act (S. 2943/P.L. 114-328 of December 23, 2016),[120] held two hearings on U.S. mobilization needs and how to meet them.[121]

DOD officials have begun to focus more on actions to improve U.S. mobilization capabilities.[122] A February 2, 2022, press report stated

> If a war against a major adversary breaks out, it's going to require the military to resupply troops at a pace it hasn't seen in a long time, Air Force Gen. Jacqueline Van Ovost, head of U.S. Transportation Command, said on Wednesday [February 2].
>
> And to keep up with that frenetic tempo, TRANSCOM is going to have to use machine learning and artificial intelligence to streamline its logistics operations, Van Ovost said in an online conversation hosted by the Center for Strategic and International Studies.
>
> "We can't afford to sift through reams and reams of data" in a major war, Van Ovost said. "We really do need to apply machine learning and artificial intelligence to turn that data into knowledge, for which we can make decisions. Creating that decision advantage is going to give us that time and space and options for senior leaders to come up with different options to reduce risk, to increase effectiveness."
>
> Van Ovost said American allies and partners, as well as its potential competitors, are already making fast progress in these areas, and the U.S. must do the same at all levels to be more effective and efficient....
>
> Van Ovost expressed interest in recent work studying the feasibility of using rockets to rapidly move large cargo loads anywhere in the world. TRANSCOM has signed research agreements with companies such as SpaceX and xArc to see how the technology might work, including cargo loading and determining flight frequency.[123]

Supply Chain Security

The emergence of GPC has led to an increased emphasis in U.S. defense planning on supply chain security, meaning (in this context) awareness and minimization of reliance in U.S. military systems on components, subcomponents, materials, and software from other countries, particularly China and Russia. An early example concerned the Russian-made RD-180 rocket engine, which was incorporated into certain U.S. space launch rockets, including rockets used by DOD to put military payloads into orbit.[124] More recent examples include the dependence of various U.S. military systems on rare earth elements from China, Chinese-made electronic

---

[120] See Sections 551 through 557 of S. 2943/P.L. 114-328.

[121] The commission's web pages for the two hearings, which include links to the prepared statements of the witnesses and additional statements submitted by other parties, are at https://inspire2serve.gov/hearings/selective-service-hearing-future-mobilization-needs-nation (hearing from 9 am to 12 noon) and https://inspire2serve.gov/hearings/selective-service-hearing-how-meet-potential-national-mobilization-needs (hearing from 1 pm to 4 pm).

[122] See, for example, Sydney J. Freedberg Jr., "WW II On Speed: Joint Staff Fears Long War," *Breaking Defense*, January 11, 2017; Department of Defense, *Assessing and Strengthening the Manufacturing and Defense Industrial Base and Supply Chain Resiliency of the United States*, September 2018, 140 pp.; Joint Chiefs of Staff, *Joint Mobilization Planning*, Joint Publication 4-05, 137 pp., October 23, 2018; Memorandum from Michael D. Griffin, Under Secretary of Defense, Research and Engineering, for Chairman, Defense Science Board, Subject: Terms of Reference—Defense Science Board Task Force on 21ˢᵗ Century Industrial Base for National Defense, October 30, 2019. See also CRS In Focus IF11311, *Defense Primer: The National Technology and Industrial Base*, by Heidi M. Peters and Luke A. Nicastro.

[123] Stephen Losey, "Data and Rockets: US Military Eyes New Tech to Supply Far-Flung Forces," *Defense News*, February 2, 2022. See also James Foggo, "How to Lose the Next War: Ignore the Supply Chain," *The Hill*, January 25, 2022.

[124] See CRS Report R44498, *National Security Space Launch at a Crossroads*, by Steven A. Hildreth.

---

components, software that may contain Chinese- or Russian-origin elements, DOD purchases of Chinese-made drones, and the use of Chinese-made surveillance cameras at U.S. military installations. The supply-chain impacts of Russia's invasion of multiple parts of Ukraine starting on February 24, 2022, have put an additional spotlight on the issue of supply chain security.[125]

A November 5, 2019, press report states

> The US navy secretary has warned that the "fragile" American supply chain for military warships means the Pentagon is at risk of having to rely on adversaries such as Russia and China for critical components.
>
> Richard Spencer, [who was then] the US navy's top civilian, told the Financial Times he had ordered a review this year that found many contractors were reliant on single suppliers for certain high-tech and high-precision parts, increasing the likelihood they would have to be procured from geostrategic rivals.
>
> Mr Spencer said the US was engaged in "great power competition" with other global rivals and that several of them—"primarily Russia and China"—were "all of a sudden in your supply chain, [which is] not to the best interests of what you're doing" through military procurement.[126]

In response to concerns like those above, DOD officials have begun to focus more on actions to improve supply chain security. On February 24, 2021, President Biden issued an executive order on strengthening the resilience of U.S. supply chains. The executive order directed a "complete a review of supply chain risks," to be completed within 100 days of the date of the executive order, and several sectoral supply chain assessments to be submitted within one year of the date of the executive order, to be followed by reports "reviewing the actions taken over the previous year and making recommendations" for additional actions.[127] In February 2022, the Biden Administration released a report on the results of the review.[128]

For a list of reports and articles on this issue, see **Appendix D**.

Capabilities for Countering Hybrid Warfare and Gray-Zone Tactics

Russia's seizure and purported annexation of Crimea in 2014, as well as subsequent Russian actions in eastern Ukraine and elsewhere in Eastern Europe and Russia's information operations, have led to a focus among policymakers on how to counter Russia's so-called hybrid warfare or ambiguous warfare tactics. China's actions in the South and East China Seas have similarly prompted a focus among policymakers on how to counter China's so-called salami-slicing or gray-zone tactics in those areas.[129] The Biden Administration's October 2022 NDS states

> *Competitors' Gray Zone Activities*. Competitors now commonly seek adverse changes in the status quo using gray zone methods—coercive approaches that may fall below perceived thresholds for U.S. military action and across areas of responsibility of different parts of the U.S. Government. The PRC employs state-controlled forces, cyber and space

---

[125] See, for example, Christian Davenport, "Russia Cuts Off Rocket Engine Supply and Threatens Space Station Partnership," *Washington Post*, March 3, 2022.

[126] Peter Spiegel and Andrew Edgecliffe-Johnson, "Us Navy Secretary Warns of 'Fragile' Supply Chain," *Financial Times*, November 5, 2019. Material in brackets as in original.

[127] White House, "Executive Order on America's Supply Chains," February 24, 2021. The executive order was number 14017.

[128] Department of Defense, *Securing Defense-Critical Supply Chains, An Action Plan Developed in Response to President Biden's Executive Order 14017*, February 2022, 74 pp.

[129] See CRS Report R42784, *U.S.-China Strategic Competition in South and East China Seas: Background and Issues for Congress*, by Ronald O'Rourke.

operations, and economic coercion against the United States and its Allies and partners. Russia employs disinformation, cyber, and space operations against the United States and our Allies and partners, and irregular proxy forces in multiple countries. Other state actors, particularly North Korea and Iran, use similar if currently more limited means. The proliferation of advanced missiles, uncrewed aircraft systems, and cyber tools to military proxies allows competitors to threaten U.S. forces, Allies, and partners, in indirect and deniable ways.[130]

For a list of articles discussing this issue, see **Appendix E**.

Issues for Congress

Potential policy and oversight issues for Congress include the following:

- **October 2022 NSS and NDS.** Do the Biden Administration's October 2022 NSS and NDS accurately describe GPC and place it in appropriate context relative to other U.S. national security concerns? Do the October 2022 NSS and NDS present an appropriate national security strategy and national defense strategy for responding to GPC?

- **U.S. grand strategy.** Should the United States continue to include, as a key element of U.S. grand strategy, a goal of preventing the emergence of a regional hegemon in one part of Eurasia or another?[131] If not, what grand strategy should the United States pursue? What is the Biden Administration's position on this issue?[132]

- **Force-planning standard.** What force-planning standard is the Biden Administration using to size U.S. military forces? Why does the October 2022 NDS not include an explicit statement of the Administration's force-planning standard? Should the United States adopt a two-war force-planning standard

---

[130] Department of Defense, *2022 National Defense Strategy of the United States of America*, cover letter dated October 27, 2022, p. 6.

[131] One observer states that this question was reviewed in 1992, at the beginning of the post–Cold War era:

> As a Pentagon planner in 1992, my colleagues and I considered seriously the idea of conceding to great powers like Russia and China their own spheres of influence, which would potentially allow the United States to collect a bigger "peace dividend" and spend it on domestic priorities.
>
> Ultimately, however, we concluded that the United States has a strong interest in precluding the emergence of another bipolar world—as in the Cold War—or a world of many great powers, as existed before the two world wars. Multipolarity led to two world wars and bipolarity resulted in a protracted worldwide struggle with the risk of nuclear annihilation. To avoid a return such circumstances, Secretary of Defense Dick Cheney ultimately agreed that our objective must be to prevent a hostile power to dominate a "critical region," which would give it the resources, industrial capabilities and population to pose a global challenge. This insight has guided U.S. defense policy throughout the post–Cold War era.
>
> (Zalmay Khalilzad, "4 Lessons about America's Role in the World," *National Interest*, March 23, 2016.)

See also Hal Brands, "Don't Let Great Powers Carve Up the World, Spheres of Influence Are Unnecessary and Dangerous," *Foreign Affairs*, April 20, 2020.

[132] The Biden Administration's October 2022 NSS states "If one region descends into chaos or is dominated by a hostile power, it will detrimentally impact our interests in the others." Regarding the Middle East, it states that "the United States will not allow foreign or regional powers to jeopardize freedom of navigation through the Middle East's waterways, including the Strait of Hormuz and the Bab al Mandab, nor tolerate efforts by any country to dominate another—or the region—through military buildups, incursions, or threats" (White House, *National Security Strategy*, October 2022, pp. 11, 42).

---

relating to potential conflicts with China and Russia? What would be the potential benefits, costs, and risks of adopting and implementing such a standard?

- **DOD organization.** Is DOD optimally organized for GPC? What further changes, if any, should be made to better to better align DOD's activities with those needed to counter Chinese and Russian military capabilities?

- **Nuclear weapons, nuclear deterrence, and nuclear arms control.** Are current DOD plans for modernizing U.S. strategic nuclear weapons, and for numbers and basing of nonstrategic (i.e., theater-range) nuclear weapons, aligned with the needs of GPC? What role can or should nuclear arms control play in a situation of GPC?

- **U.S. global military posture.** Should U.S. global military posture be altered, and if so, how? What are the potential benefits and risks of shifting U.S. military capabilities and force deployments out of some areas and into others? Should the Biden Administration's proposals for the global distribution of U.S. military force deployments be approved, rejected, or modified?

- **U.S. and allied military capabilities in the Indo-Pacific region.** Are the United States and its allies in the Indo-Pacific region taking appropriate and sufficient steps for countering China's military capabilities in the Indo-Pacific region? To what degree will countering China's military capabilities in the Indo-Pacific region require reductions in U.S. force deployments to other parts of the world?

- **U.S. and NATO military capabilities in Europe.** Are the United States and its NATO allies taking appropriate and sufficient steps regarding U.S. and NATO military capabilities and operations for countering potential Russian military aggression in parts of Europe other than Ukraine? What potential impacts would a strengthened U.S. military presence in Europe have on DOD's ability to allocate additional U.S. forces to the Indo-Pacific region? To what degree can or should the NATO allies in Europe take actions to strengthen deterrence against potential Russian aggression in parts of Europe other than Ukraine?

- **New operational concepts.** Are U.S. military services moving too slowly, too quickly, or at about the right speed in their efforts to develop new operational concepts in response to the emergence of GPC, particularly against improving Chinese anti-access/area-denial (A2/AD) forces? What are the potential merits of these new operational concepts, and what steps are the services taking in terms of experiments and exercises to test and refine these concepts? To what degree are the services working to coordinate and integrate their new operational concepts on a cross-service basis?

- **Capabilities for high-end conventional warfare.** Are DOD's plans for acquiring capabilities for high-end conventional warfare appropriate and sufficient? In a situation of finite defense resources, how should trade-offs be made in balancing capabilities for high-end conventional warfare against other DOD priorities?

- **Maintaining U.S. superiority in conventional weapon technologies.** Are DOD's steps for maintaining U.S. superiority in conventional weapon technologies appropriate and sufficient? What impact will funding these technologies have on funding available for nearer-term DOD priorities, such as maintaining U.S. force structure (i.e., numbers of military units) or redressing deficiencies in force readiness?

- **Innovation and speed in weapon system development and deployment.** To what degree should defense acquisition policy and the paradigm for assessing the success of acquisition programs be adjusted to place greater emphasis on innovation and speed of development and deployment, and on experimentation, risk taking, and greater tolerance of failure during development? Are DOD's steps for doing this appropriate and sufficient? What new legislative authorities, if any, might be required (or what existing provisions, if any, might need to be amended or repealed) to achieve greater innovation and speed in weapon development and deployment? What implications might placing a greater emphasis on speed of acquisition have on familiar congressional paradigms for conducting oversight and judging the success of defense acquisition programs?

- **Mobilization capabilities.** What actions is DOD taking regarding mobilization capabilities for an extended-length conflict against an adversary such as China or Russia, and are these actions appropriate? What are current industrial capacity limits for producing key weapons and equipment, including precision-guided munitions? How quickly could industrial capacity for producing key weapons and equipment be increased, and how much would it cost to create the additional production capacity? More generally, how much funding is being devoted to mobilization capabilities, and how are mobilization capabilities projected to change as a result of these actions in coming years?

- **Supply chain security.** To what degree are Chinese or Russian components, subcomponents, materials, or software incorporated into DOD equipment? How good of an understanding does DOD have of this issue? What implications might this issue have for the effectiveness, reliability, maintainability, and reparability of U.S. military systems, particularly in time of war? What actions is DOD taking or planning to take to address supply chain security, particularly with regard to Chinese or Russian components, subcomponents, materials, and software? What impact might this issue have on U.S.-content requirements (aka Buy America requirements) for U.S. military systems?

- **Hybrid warfare and gray-zone tactics.** Do the United States and its allies and partners have adequate strategies for countering Russia's so-called hybrid warfare in eastern Ukraine, Russia's information operations, and China's so-called salami-slicing tactics in the South and East China Seas?

Appendix A. Transition from Post–Cold War Era to GPC

This appendix presents additional background information on the transition from the post–Cold War era to GPC. For a list of articles on this shift, see **Appendix B**.

Previous International Security Environments

Cold War Era

The Cold War era of international relations is generally viewed as having lasted from the late 1940s until the late 1980s or early 1990s and is generally characterized as having been a strongly bipolar situation in which two superpowers—the United States and the Soviet Union—engaged, along with their allies, in a political, ideological, and military competition for influence across multiple geographic regions. The military component of that competition was often most acutely visible in Europe, where the U.S.-led NATO alliance and the Soviet-led Warsaw Pact alliance faced off against one another with large numbers of conventional forces and theater nuclear weapons, backed by longer-ranged strategic nuclear weapons.

Post–Cold War Era

The post–Cold War era is generally viewed as having begun in the late 1980s and early 1990s, following the fall of the Berlin Wall in November 1989, the disbanding of the Soviet-led Warsaw Pact military alliance in March 1991, and the dissolution of the Soviet Union into Russia and the former Soviet republics in December 1991, which were key events marking the ending of the Cold War. Compared to the Cold War, the post–Cold War era is generally characterized as having featured reduced levels of overt political, ideological, and military competition among major states.

The post–Cold War era is also sometimes characterized as having tended toward a unipolar situation, with the United States as the world's sole superpower. Neither Russia, China, nor any other country was viewed as posing a significant challenge to either the United States' status as the world's sole superpower or the U.S.-led international order. Following the terrorist attacks of September 11, 2001 (aka 9/11), the post–Cold War era was additionally characterized by a strong focus (at least from a U.S. perspective) on countering transnational terrorist organizations that had emerged as significant non-state actors, particularly Al Qaeda.

Great Power Competition

Overview

The post–Cold War era showed initial signs of fading in 2006-2008 (see "Markers of Shift to GPC" below). By 2014—following Chinese actions in the South and East China Seas[133] and Russia's seizure and annexation of Crimea[134]—the post–Cold War era was viewed as having

---

[133] For discussions of these actions, see CRS Report R42784, *U.S.-China Strategic Competition in South and East China Seas: Background and Issues for Congress*, by Ronald O'Rourke, and CRS Report R42930, *Maritime Territorial Disputes in East Asia: Issues for Congress*, by Ben Dolven, Mark E. Manyin, and Shirley A. Kan.

[134] For discussion Russia's seizure and annexation of Crimea, see CRS Report R45008, *Ukraine: Background, Conflict* (continued...)

---

given way to a new situation, often referred to as great power competition, of intensified U.S. competition with China and Russia, as well as challenges by those two countries and others to elements of the U.S.-led international order established after World War II.

Some Key Apparent Features

Observers view GPC not as a bipolar situation (like the Cold War) or a unipolar situation (like the post–Cold War era) but as a situation characterized in substantial part by renewed competition among three major world powers—the United States, China, and Russia. Key apparent features of the current situation of GPC include (but are not necessarily limited to) the following:

- renewed ideological competition, this time against 21st-century forms of authoritarianism and illiberal democracy in Russia, China, and other countries;

- competition for allies and partner states;

- technological competition, particularly between the United States and China;

- the promotion by China and Russia of nationalistic historical narratives,[135] some emphasizing assertions of prior humiliation or victimization by Western powers, and the use of those narratives to support revanchist or irredentist foreign policy aims;

- challenges by Russia and China to key elements of the U.S.-led international order, including the unacceptability of changing international borders by force or coercion and a preference for resolving disputes between countries peacefully without the use or threat of use of force or coercion;

- the use by Russia and China of new forms of aggressive or assertive military, paramilitary, information, and cyber operations—sometimes called hybrid warfare, gray-zone operations, or ambiguous warfare, among other terms, in the case of Russia's actions and salami-slicing tactics or gray-zone operations, among other terms, in the case of China's actions; and

- additional features alongside those listed above, including

  - continued regional security challenges from countries such as Iran and North Korea;

  - a continued focus (at least from a U.S. perspective) on countering transnational terrorist organizations that emerge as significant non-state actors; and

  - weak or failed states, and resulting weakly governed or ungoverned areas that can contribute to the emergence of (or serve as base areas or sanctuaries for) non-state actors, and become potential locations of intervention by stronger states, including major powers.

Markers of Shift to GPC

The sharpest single marker of the transition from the post–Cold War era to GPC arguably was Russia's seizure and annexation of Crimea in March 2014, which represented the first forcible seizure and annexation of one country's territory by another country in Europe since World War

---

with Russia, and U.S. Policy, by Cory Welt, and CRS Report R44775, *Russia: Background and U.S. Policy*, by Cory Welt.

[135] See for example, Jessica Chen Weiss, "The Stories China Tells: The New Historical Memory Reshaping Chinese Nationalism," *Foreign Affairs*, March/April 2021.

AI-42

II. Other markers of the shift—such as China's economic growth and military modernization and China's actions in the South and East China Seas—were more gradual and cumulative.

The beginnings of the transition from the post–Cold War era to GPC can be traced to the period 2006-2008:

- Freedom House's annual report on freedom in the world states that, by the organization's own analysis, countries experiencing net declines in freedom have outnumbered countries experiencing net increases in freedom every year since in 2006.[136]

- In February 2007, in a speech at an international security conference in Munich, Russian President Vladimir Putin criticized and rejected the concept of a unipolar power, predicted a shift to multipolar order, and affirmed an active Russian role in international affairs. Some observers view the speech in retrospect as prefiguring a more assertive and competitive Russian foreign policy.[137]

- In 2008, Russia invaded and occupied part of the former Soviet republic of Georgia without provoking a strong cost-imposing response from the United States and its allies.[138] Also in that year, the financial crisis and resulting deep recessions in the United States and Europe, combined with China's ability to weather that crisis and its successful staging of the 2008 Summer Olympics, are seen by observers as having contributed to a perception in China of the United States as a declining power, and to a Chinese sense of self-confidence or triumphalism.[139] China's assertive actions in the South and East China Seas can be viewed as having begun (or accelerated) soon thereafter.

Other observers trace the roots of the transition to GPC further to years prior to 2006-2008.[140]

---

[136] See, for example, Sarah Repucci, General Editor, *Freedom in the World 2020, The Annual Survey of Political Rights & Civil Liberties*, Freedom House, 2021, p. 2.

[137] For an English-language transcript of the speech, see "Putin's Prepared Remarks at 43rd Munich Conference on Security Policy," Washington Post, accessed January 25, 2022, at https://www.washingtonpost.com/wp-dyn/content/article/2007/02/12/AR2007021200555.html. See also Ted Galen Carpenter, "Did Putin's 2007 Munich Speech Predict the Ukraine Crisis?" *National Interest*, January 24, 2022; Rakesh Sood, "Putin is Forcing a Third Reordering of Europe," *Observer Research Foundation*, February 9, 2022; Daniel Fried and Kurt Volker, "The Speech In Which Putin Told Us Who He Was, In His 2007 Munich Address, the Russian Leader Firmly Rejected the Post-Cold War System He's Still Trying to Torpedo," *Politico*, February 18, 2022; David Ignatius, "Putin Warned the West 15 Years Ago. Now, in Ukraine, He's Poised to Wage War," *Washington Post*, February 20, 2022; Michael R. Gordon, Stephen Fidler, and Alan Cullison, "How the West Misread Vladimir Putin, The Former KGB Officer Spent Years Assailing the Post-Cold War Order and Sent Repeated Signals He Intended to Widen Russia's Sphere Of Influence," *Wall Street Journal*, February 25, 2022. See also Kim Ghattas, "What a Decade-Old Conflict Tells Us About Putin, One Can Trace a Straight Line from the Overthrow of Libya's Dictator Muammar Gaddafi to Today's Devastating War in Ukraine," *Atlantic*, March 6, 2022.

[138] See, for example, Robert Kagan, "Believe It or Not, Trump's Following a Familiar Script on Russia," *Washington Post,* August 7, 2018. For a response, see Condoleezza Rice, "Russia Invaded Georgia 10 Years Ago. Don't Say America Didn't Respond." *Washington Post*, August 8, 2018. See also Ben Smith, "U.S. Pondered Military Use in Georgia," *Politico*, February 3, 2010; Mikheil Saakashvili, "When Russia Invaded Georgia," *Wall Street Journal*, August 7, 2018; Lahav Harkov, "2 Years On, Georgian Ambassador Sees War with Russia as Warning to Europe," *Jerusalem Post*, August 5, 2020; Rakesh Sood, "Putin is Forcing a Third Reordering of Europe," *Observer Research Foundation*, February 9, 2022.

[139] See, for example, Howard W. French, "China's Dangerous Game," *Atlantic*, October 13, 2014.

[140] See, for example, David Ignatius, "The Moment when Putin Turned Away from the West," *Washington Post*, March 9, 2023; Paul Blustein, "The Untold Story of How George W. Bush Lost China," *Foreign Policy*, October 2, 2019; Walter Russell Mead, "Who's to Blame for a World in Flames?" *The American Interest*, October 6, 2014; Robert (continued...)

Comparisons to Past International Security Environments

Some observers seek to better understand the current situation of GPC in part by comparing it to past international security environments. Each international security environment features its own combination of major actors, dimensions of competition and cooperation among those actors, and military and other technologies available to them. A given international security environment can have some similarities to previous ones, but it will also have differences, including, potentially, one or more features not present in any other international security environment. In the early years of a new international security environment, some of its features may be unclear, in dispute, not yet apparent, or subject to evolution. In attempting to understand an international security environment, comparisons to other ones are potentially helpful in identifying avenues of investigation. If applied too rigidly, however, such comparisons can act as intellectual straightjackets, making it more difficult to achieve a full understanding of a given international security environment's characteristic features, particularly those that differentiate it from previous ones.[141]

Some observers are describing the current situation of GPC as a new Cold War (or Cold War II or 2.0), particularly since Russia's invasion of multiple parts of Ukraine starting on February 24, 2022. That term may have utility in referring specifically to current U.S.-Russian or U.S.-Chinese relations. The original Cold War, however, was a bipolar situation with the United States and Russia, while the current situation of GPC is a three-power situation involving the United States, China, and Russia. The bipolarity of the Cold War, moreover, was reinforced by the opposing NATO and Warsaw Pact alliances, whereas in contrast, neither Russia nor China today lead an equivalent of the Warsaw Pact. And while terrorists were a concern during the Cold War, the U.S. focus on countering transnational terrorist groups was not nearly as significant during the original Cold War as it has been since 9/11.

Other observers, viewing the emergence of GPC, have drawn comparisons to the multipolar situation that existed in the 19th century or the years prior to World War I. Still others, observing the promotion in China and Russia of nationalistic historical narratives supporting revanchist or irredentist foreign policy aims, China's military modernization, and Russia-China strategic cooperation, have drawn comparisons to the 1930s.[142] The military and other technologies available in those earlier situations, however, differ vastly from those available today. The current situation of GPC may be similar in some respects to previous situations, but it also differs from previous situations in certain respects, and might be best understood by direct observation and identification of its key features.

Kagan, "End of Dreams, Return of History," *Policy Review (Hoover Institution)*, July 17, 2007. See also Thomas P. Ehrhard, "Treating the Pathologies of Victory: Hardening the Nation for Strategic Competition," p. 23, in *2020 Index of U.S. Military Strength*, Heritage Foundation, 2020; Michael Rubin, "Russia Was a Rogue State Long Before Ukraine and Georgia," American Enterprise Institute, February 18, 2022; Jade McGlynn, "Why Putin Keeps Talking About Kosovo, For the Kremlin, NATO's 1999 War Against Serbia Is the West's Original Sin—and a Humiliating Affront that Russia Must Avenge," *Foreign Policy*, March 3, 2022.

[141] See, for example, Christopher David LaRoche, "Ukraine Isn't Munich—or Vietnam or Berlin," *Foreign Policy*, October 15, 2022; Josh Kerbel, "By Calling It a 'Cold War' We Risk Containing Ourselves," *The Hill*, October 3, 2022; Jonah Goldberg, "A Tale of Two Cold Wars, The Differences between the Cold War Era and Today Are Profound," *Dispatch*, March 16, 2022; Ross Douthat, "The Ukraine War and the Retro-Future," *New York Times*, March 12, 2022.

[142] See, for example, Gideon Rachman, "China, Japan and the Ukraine War, The Merging of Geopolitical rivalries in Asia and Europe Has Disturbing Echoes of the 1930s," *Financial Times*, March 27, 2023.

Naming the Current Situation

Observers viewing the current situation have given it various names, but names using some variation of great power competition or renewed great power competition appear to have become the most commonly used in public policy discussions. As noted earlier, some observers are using the term Cold War (or New Cold War, or Cold War II or 2.0), particularly since Russia's invasion of multiple parts of Ukraine starting on February 24, 2022. Other terms that have been used include competitive world order, multipolar era, tripolar era, and disorderly world (or era), and strategic competition.

Congress and the Previous Shift

The previous major change in the international security environment—the transition in the late 1980s and early 1990s from the Cold War to the post–Cold War era—prompted a broad reassessment by DOD and Congress of defense funding levels, strategy, and missions that led to numerous changes in DOD plans and programs. Many of these changes were articulated in the 1993 Bottom-Up Review (BUR),[143] a reassessment of U.S. defense plans and programs whose very name conveyed the fundamental nature of the reexamination that had occurred.[144] In general, the BUR reshaped the U.S. military into a force that was smaller than the Cold War U.S. military, and oriented toward a planning scenario being able to conduct two major regional contingencies (MRCs) rather than the Cold War planning scenario of a NATO-Warsaw Pact conflict.[145] For additional discussion of Congress's response to the shift from the Cold War to the post–Cold War era, see **Appendix F**.

---

[143] See Department of Defense, *Report on the Bottom-Up Review*, Les Aspin, Secretary of Defense, October 1993, 109 pp.

[144] Secretary of Defense Les Aspin's introduction to DOD's report on the 1993 BUR states the following:

> In March 1993, I initiated a comprehensive review of the nation's defense strategy, force structure, modernization, infrastructure, and foundations. I felt that a department-wide review needed to be conducted "from the bottom up" because of the dramatic changes that have occurred in the world as a result of the end of the Cold War and the dissolution of the Soviet Union. These changes in the international security environment have fundamentally altered America's security needs. Thus, the underlying premise of the Bottom-Up Review was that we needed to reassess all of our defense concepts, plans, and programs from the ground up.

> (Department of Defense, *Report on the Bottom-Up Review*, Les Aspin, Secretary of Defense, October 1993, p. iii.)

[145] For additional discussion of the results of the BUR, see CRS Report 93-839 F, *Defense Department Bottom-Up Review: Results and Issues*, October 6, 1993, 6 pp., by Edward F. Bruner, and CRS Report 93-627 F, *Defense Department Bottom-Up Review: The Process*, July 2, 1993, 9 pp., by Cedric W. Tarr Jr. (both nondistributable and available to congressional clients from CRS).

Appendix B. Articles on Transition to GPC and GPC in General

This appendix presents citations to articles about the transition from the post–Cold War era to GPC and about GPC in general.

Citation from 2007

Robert Kagan, "End of Dreams, Return of History," *Policy Review (Hoover Institution)*, July 17, 2007.

Citations from Late-2013 and 2014

Walter Russell Mead, "The End of History Ends," *The American Interest*, December 2, 2013.

Paul David Miller, "Crimea Proves That Great Power Rivalry Never Left Us," *Foreign Policy*, March 21, 2014.

Stephen M. Walt, "The Bad Old Days Are Back," *Foreign Policy*, May 2, 2014.

Walter Russell Mead, "The Return of Geopolitics," *Foreign Affairs*, May/June 2014.

Robert Kagan, "Superpowers Don't Get to Retire," *New Republic*, May 26, 2014.

James Kitfield, "The New Great Power Triangle Tilt: China, Russia Vs. U.S.," *Breaking Defense*, June 19, 2014.

Lilia Shevtsova, "Putin Ends the Interregnum," *The American Interest*, August 28, 2014.

David E. Sanger, "Commitments on Three Fronts Test Obama's Foreign Policy," *New York Times*, September 3, 2014.

Steven Erlanger, "NATO's Hopes for Russia Have Turned to Dismay," *New York Times*, September 12, 2014.

Richard N. Haass, "The Era of Disorder," *Project Syndicate*, October 27, 2014.

Citations from January through June 2015

Bruce Jones, "What Strategic Environment Does the Transatlantic Community Confront?" German Marshall Fund of the United States, Policy Brief, January 15, 2015, 5 pp.

Chester A Crocker, "The Strategic Dilemma of a World Adrift," *Survival*, February-March 2015: 7-30.

Robert Kagan, "The United States Must Resist A Return to Spheres of Interest in in the International System," Brookings Institution, February 19, 2015.

Richard Fontaine, "Salvaging Global Order," *The National Interest*, March 10, 2015.

Barry Pavel and Peter Engelke with Alex Ward, *Dynamic Stability, US Strategy for a World in Transition*, Washington, Atlantic Council, April 2015, 57 pp.

Stewart Patrick and Isabella Bennett, "Geopolitics Is Back—and Global Governance Is Out," *The National Interest*, May 12, 2015.

"Rise of the Regional Hegemons," *Wall Street Journal*, May 25, 2015.

Frank G. Hoffman and Ryan Neuhard, "Is the World Getting Safer—or Not?" Foreign Policy Research Institute, June 2015.

Citations from July through December 2015

James Kitfield, "Requiem For The Obama Doctrine," *Breaking Defense*, July 6, 2015.

Mathew Burrows and Robert A. Manning, "America's Worst Nightmare: Russia and China Are Getting Closer," *National Interest*, August 24, 2015.

Robert Farley, "Yes, America's Military Supremacy Is Fading (And We Should Not Panic)," *National Interest*, September 21, 2015.

John McLaughlin, "The Geopolitical Rules You Didn't Know About Are Under Siege," *Ozy*, November 10, 2015.

Citations from January through June 2016

John E. McLaughlin, "US Strategy and Strategic Culture from 2017," *Global Brief*, February 19, 2016.

H.R. McMaster, "Probing for Weakness," *Wall Street Journal*, March 23, 2016.

Zbigniew Brzezinski, "Toward a Global Realignment," *The American Interest*, April 17, 2016.

Michael J. Boyle, "The Coming Illiberal Order," *Survival*, Vol. 58, April-May 2016: 35-66.

Kurt Campbell et al., *Extending American Power*, Center for a New American Security (CNAS), May 2016, 18 pp.

Michael Mandelbaum, "America in a New World," *The American Interest*, May 23, 2016.

Citations from July through December 2016

Michael Lind, "Can America Share Its Superpower Status?" *National Interest*, August 21, 2016.

Bret Stephens, "The New Dictators' Club," *Wall Street Journal*, August 22, 2016.

Gregory R. Copley, "The Era of Strategic Containment is Over," *Defense & Foreign Affairs*, September 7, 2016.

Ulrich Speck, "The Crisis of Liberal Order," *American Interest*, September 12, 2016.

Aaron Kliegman, "Robert D. Kaplan: Think Tragically to Avoid Tragedy," *Washington Free Beacon*, September 16, 2016.

Lauren Villagran, "Former Defense Secretary Describes 'New World Order,'" *Stars and Stripes*, September 14, 2016.

George F. Will, "Vladimir Putin Is Bringing Back the 1930s," *Washington Post*, October 7, 2016.

Philip Stephens, "How the West Has Lost the World," *Financial Times*, October 12, 2016.

John Sawers, "We Are Returning to a World of Great-Power Rivalry," *Financial Times*, October 19, 2016.

Patrick Wintour, Luke Harding, and Julian Borger, "Cold War 2.0: How Russia and the West Reheated a Historic Struggle," *The Guardian*, October 24, 2016.

John Schaus, "U.S. Leadership in an Era of Great Power Competition," *Defense 360* (Center for Strategic and International Studies [CSIS]), December 2016.

Charles Krauthammer, "After a Mere 25 Years, the Triumph of the West Is Over," *Washington Post*, December 1, 2016.

Julia Ioffe, "The End of the End of the Cold War," *Foreign Policy*, December 21, 2016.

Citations from January through June 2017

Richard Haass, "World Order 2.0," *Foreign Affairs*, January/February 2017: 2-9.

Joseph S. Nye Jr., "Will the Liberal Order Survive," *Foreign Affairs*, January/February 2017: 10-16.

Molly K. McKew, "Putin's Real Long Game," *Politico Magazine*, January 1, 2017.

Robert J. Samuelson, "The New World Order, 2017," *Washington Post*, January 1, 2017.

Martin Wolf, "Martin Wolf: The Long and Painful Journey to World Disorder," *Financial Times*, January 5, 2017.

Kimberly Dozier, "U.S. Spies See a World of Trumps Ahead," *Daily Beast*, January 9, 2017.

Kenneth Roth, "We Are on the Verge of Darkness," *Foreign Policy*, January 12, 2017.

Thomas Donnelly, "Now for the Post-Post-Cold War Era," *Weekly Standard*, January 23, 2017.

Evan Osnos, David Remnick, and Joshua Yaffa, "Trump, Putin, and the New Cold War," *New Yorker*, March 6, 2017.

Paul Berman, "The Counterrevolution," *Tablet*, March 7, 2017.

James Kirchick, "The Road to a Free Europe Goes Through Moscow," *Politico Magazine*, March 17, 2017.

Andrew A. Michta, "The Deconstruction of the West," *American Interest*, April 12, 2017.

Michael Mazarr and Hal Brands, "Navigating Great Power Rivalry in the 21st Century," *War on the Rocks*, April 5, 2017.

Robert D. Kaplan, "The Return of Marco Polo's World and the U.S. Military Response," CNAS, undated but posted ca. May 12, 2017.

Hal Brands and Eric Edelman, "America and the Geopolitics of Upheaval," *National Interest*, June 21, 2017.

Christopher Walker, "A New Era of Competition," International Reports (Konrad Adenauer Foundation), No. 2, 2017: 16-25.

Citations from July 2017 through December 2017

Hal Brands, Charles Edel, "The Gathering Storm vs. the Crisis of Confidence," *Foreign Policy*, July 14, 2017.

Leon Hadar, "Why Washington's Global Strategy Failed," *National Interest*, July 30, 2017.

Paul Mason, "Democracy Is Dying—and It's Startling How Few People Are Worried," *The Guardian*, July 31, 2017.

Harvey M. Sapolsky, "America's Endless Search for a Strategy," *National Interest*, August 4, 2017.

Philip Zelikow, "Is the World Slouching Toward a Grave Systemic Crisis?" *Atlantic*, August 11, 2017.

Robert D. Kaplan, "America's Darwinian Nationalism," *National Interest*, August 13, 2017.

He Yafei, "The 'American Century' Has Come to Its End," *Global Times*, August 20, 2017.

He Yafei, "New World Order is the Inevitable Trend," *China Daily*, August 21, 2017.

Michael Lind, "There's No Such Thing as 'The' Liberal World Order," *National Interest*, September 5, 2017.

Thorsten Benner, "An Era of Authoritarian Influence? How Democracies Should Respond," *Foreign Affairs*, September 15, 2017.

Hal Brands, "America's New World Order Is Officially Dead," *Bloomberg*, September 27, 2017.

Andrew A. Michta, "The Crisis of Elite Authority in the West," *American Interest*, September 27, 2017.

Erica Frantz and Andrea Kendall-Taylor, "The Evolution of Autocracy: Why Authoritarianism Is Becoming More Formidable," *Survival*, October-November 2017: 57-68.

Larry Diamond, "Is There a Crisis of Liberal democracy?" *American Interest*, October 13, 2017.

Colin Dueck and Ming Wan, "An Era of Great-Power Leaders," *National Interest*, November 7, 2017.

Brendan Nicholson, "The Strategist Six: Thomas Mahnken," *Strategist (ASPI)*, November 7, 2017. (Interview with Thomas Mahnken.)

Citations from January 2018 through December 2020

"The Growing Danger of Great-Power Conflict," *Economist*, January 25, 2018.

Alan Dupont, "New World Order: Momentum Is Shifting in Favour of Dictators," *Australian*, February 10, 2018.

Gabriel Glickman, "Back to the Future: The Potential of Great-Power Conflict," *National Interest*, February 12, 2018.

Eliot A. Cohen, "Witnessing the Collapse of the Global Elite," *Atlantic*, February 19, 2018.

Hal Brands, "The 'American Century' Is Over, and It Died in Syria," *Bloomberg*, March 8, 2018.

Richard N. Haass, "Liberal World Order, RIP," *Strategist (ASPI)*, March 24, 2018.

Michael Lind, "America vs. Russia and China: Welcome to Cold War II," *National Interest*, April 15, 2018.

Nick Danforth, "What's So Disordered About Your World Order?" *War on the Rocks*, June 20, 2018.

Thomas P. Ehrhard, "Treating the Pathologies of Victory: Hardening the Nation for Strategic Competition," Heritage Foundation, October 30, 2019.

Fred Kaplan, "The Decade Big Power Politics Returned," *Slate*, December 16, 2019.

Elbridge A. Colby and A. Wess Mitchell, "The Age of Great-Power Competition," *Foreign Affairs*, January/February 2020.

Lionel Beehner and Liam Collins, Dangerous Myths, *How the Crisis in Ukraine Explains Future Great Power Conflict*, Modern War Institute at West Point, August 18, 2020, 69 pp.

Citations from January 2021 through December 2021

Ian Ona Johnson, "How an International Order Died: Lessons from the Interwar Era," *War on the Rocks*, August 5, 2021.

Mark N. Katz, "Great Power Clashes Will Reshape America, The End of the U.S.-Dominated Unipolar World Order Is Something that Has Been Predicted—Even Advocated—for Many Years," *National Interest*, August 7, 2021.

Thomas Wright, "Putin Is Taking a Huge Gamble, His Decision to Assemble an Invasion Force Along Russia's Border with Ukraine Suggests that We Are About to Enter a Dangerous New Phase of International Relations," *Atlantic*, December 10, 2021.

Citations from January 2022 through June 2022

Tom McTague, "Vladimir Putin Is a Product of Modernity, Why the Tension in Ukraine May Feel Deceptively Regressive," *Atlantic*, February 9, 2022.

Rakesh Sood, "Putin is Forcing a Third Reordering of Europe," Observer Research Foundation, February 9, 2022.

Michael Beckley, "Enemies of My Enemy, How Fear of China Is Forging a New World Order," *Foreign Affairs*, March/April 2022 (posted online February 14, 2022).

Nicole Grajewski, "An Illusory Entente: The Myth Of A Russia-China-Iran 'Axis,'" *Asian Affairs*, February 14, 2022.

Eldad Shavit and Shimon Stein, "Crisis in Ukraine: Another Effort by President Putin to Change the Existing Order in the Face of Western Determination to Preserve It," Institute for National Security Studies (INSS) (Israel), February 14, 2022.

Jun Kumakura, "Deepening Russia-China Relations—Russia's Growing Presence," Japan Institute of International Affairs (JIIA), February 16, 2022

David Brooks, "The Dark Century," *New York Times*, February 17, 2022.

Oded Eran and Zvi Magen, "Russia and China: On the Same Side in Cold War 2.0," INSS (Israel), February 17, 2022.

Veerle Nouwens and Emily Ferris, "The Beijing–Moscow Partnership: Natural or by Necessity?" Royal United Services Institute (RUSI), February 17, 2022.

Max Fisher, "Putin's Baseless Claims of Genocide Hint at More Than War, The Invocations Serve to Justify Not Just Moscow's Actions in Ukraine, but Also Its Wider Quest for a New Imperial Identity Rooted in Russian Ethnicity," *New York Times*, February 19, 2022.

Daniel Fried and Kurt Volker, "The Speech In Which Putin Told Us Who He Was, In His 2007 Munich Address, the Russian Leader Firmly Rejected the Post-Cold War System He's Still Trying to Torpedo," *Politico*, February 18, 2022.

Michael Auslin, "China and Russia Are an Alliance of Disruptors," *Spectator (UK)*, February 19, 2022.

Max Fisher, "Putin's Baseless Claims of Genocide Hint at More Than War, The Invocations Serve to Justify Not Just Moscow's Actions in Ukraine, but Also Its Wider Quest for a New Imperial Identity Rooted in Russian Ethnicity," *New York Times*, February 19, 2022.

Anton Troianovski, "In Ukraine Crisis, the Looming Threat of a New Cold War," *New York Times*, February 19, 2022.

Robin Wright, "Does the U.S.-Russia Crisis Over Ukraine Prove That the Cold War Never Ended? Putin's Aggression in Europe Has Triggered a New Debate about Whether American Presidents and Policymakers Have Misunderstood Decades of History," *New Yorker*, February 19, 2022.

David Ignatius, "Putin Warned the West 15 Years Ago. Now, in Ukraine, He's Poised to Wage War," *Washington Post*, February 20, 2022.

Douglas E. Schoen, "The Risks and Implications of China and Russia's Unholy Alliance," *The Hill*, February 20, 2022.

Farah Stockman, "This Is the Russia-China Friendship That Nixon Feared," *New York Times*, February 20, 2022.

Edward Wong, "Bond Between China and Russia Alarms U.S. and Europe Amid Ukraine Crisis," *New York Times*, February 20, 2022.

Gerard Baker, "How the U.S. and Europe Lost the Post-Cold War, Victory Bred Complacency, Neglect of Fellow Citizens, and a Failure to Preserve Our Civilizational Values," *Wall Street Journal*, February 21, 2022.

Bryan Bender and Paul McLeary, "'Cold War, Part 2': How Putin Is Dragging America Back to the Bad Old Days," *Politico Pro*, February 21, 2022.

Finbarr Bermingham, "As Ukraine Crisis Worsens, Europe Pushes Back Against China-Russia Efforts to 'Redefine' Post-War Order," *South China Morning Post*, February 21, 2022.

Tom Nichols, "Putin Chooses a Forever War, His Partition of Ukraine Is An Attack on Global Peace," *Atlantic*, February 21, 2022.

Roger Cohen, "The Limits of a Europe Whole and Free, Vladimir Putin Sets Down a Marker in Ukraine. Does the West Have the Means to Stop Him?" *New York Times*, February 22, 2022.

Editorial Board, "The '80s Got Their Foreign Policy Back, Romney Was Right About Putin in 2012, as Biden Is Learning the Hard Way," *Wall Street Journal*, February 22, 2022.

Editorial Board, "With Russia's Invasion of Ukraine, a New Cold War Arrives," *Wall Street Journal*, February 22, 2022.

Stephen Fidler, "Putin's Endgame: Unravel the Post-Cold War Agreements That Humiliated Russia," *Wall Street Journal*, February 22, 2022.

William A. Galston, "Ukraine Invasion Marks an Era's End, No One Can Deny Any Longer That Force Is a Permanent Feature of Foreign Relations," *Wall Street Journal*, February 22, 2022.

Erica Gaston, "The Russia-Ukraine Crisis Has Removed All Doubt. We're in a New Cold War," *World Politics Review*, February 22, 2022.

Hugh Hewitt, "The World Is Awake to China's and Russia's Malign Ambitions," *Washington Post*, February 22, 2022.

Holman W. Jenkins Jr., "Containing Russia, Old School," *Wall Street Journal*, February 22, 2022.

Frederick W. Kagan, "Putin Has Changed the World—and the US Must Adapt or Lose," *The Hill*, February 22, 2022.

Riccardo Alcaro, "Europe's Post-Cold War Order Is No More," Istituto Affari Internazionali (Italy), February 23, 2022.

David Brunnstrom and Michael Martina, "U.S. Says China and Russia Seek 'Profoundly Illiberal' World Order," *Reuters*, February 23, 2022.

Michael R. Gordon, "Ukraine Crisis Kicks Off New Superpower Struggle Among U.S., Russia and China," *Wall Street Journal*, February 23, 2022.

Greg Ip, "Clash Over Ukraine Drives a Dagger Into Globalization," *Wall Street Journal*, February 23, 2022.

Emma Ashford, "It's Official: The Post-Cold War Era Is Over," *New York Times*, February 24, 2022.

Stephen Blank, "The West Needs Containment 2.0," *The Hill*, February 24, 2022.

Karen DeYoung, John Hudson and Michael Birnbaum, "With Russia Attack, U.S., Europe Ponder the Future of the Post-War World They Created," *Washington Post*, February 24, 2022.

Editorial Board, "Mr. Putin Launches a Sequel to the Cold War," *New York Times*, February 24, 2022.

Editorial Board, "Putin's New World Disorder," *Wall Street Journal*, February 24, 2022.

Oona Hathaway and Scott Shapiro, "Putin Can't Destroy the International Order by Himself," Lawfare, February 24, 2022.

David Ignatius, "Putin's Assault on Ukraine Will Shape a New World Order," *Washington Post*, February 24, 2022.

Walter Russell Mead, "A Rogue Russia Tries to Reset the World Order," *Wall Street Journal*, February 24, 2022.

Gerald F. Seib, "Russia's Strike Changes Not Just Ukraine But the World, Moscow's Military Push Has Upended Post-Cold War Security, United NATO Allies and Renewed Foreign-Policy Debates," *Wall Street Journal*, February 24, 2022.

Ann M. Simmons and Matthew Luxmoore, "Ukraine Invasion Is Putin's Most Aggressive Move Yet to Restore Russia's Place in the World," *Wall Street Journal*, February 24, 2022.

Geoffrey Aronson, "The War to Reshape European Security Has Begun," *National Interest*, February 25, 2022.

Hal Brands, "The Eurasian Nightmare, Chinese-Russian Convergence and the Future of American Order," *Foreign Affairs*, February 25, 2022.

Tom McTague, "Bury the Old World Order, The Old Ways of Dealing with Russia No Longer Apply," *Atlantic*, February 25, 2022.

Ana Palacio, "Not Just Ukraine: Putin Wants to Remake the World," *Atlantic Council*, February 25, 2022.

David L. Phillips, "Contending With the New Russian Empire," *National Interest*, February 25, 2022.

David E. Sanger, "Biden Targets Russia With Strategy of Containment, Updated for a New Era," *New York Times*, February 25, 2022.

Michael Shoebridge, "Ukraine Invasion a Crystallising Moment for a More Dangerous, Divided World," *Strategist* (ASPI), February 25, 2022.

Bryan Walsh, "The War in Ukraine Could Portend the End of the 'Long Peace,'" *Vox*, February 26, 2022.

Ivan Krastev, "We Are All Living in Vladimir Putin's World Now," *New York Times*, February 27, 2022.

Jeremy Shapiro, "Why the West's China Challenge Just Got a Lot Harder, China Remains an Enormous Problem, and Russia's Invasion of Ukraine Only Makes It Worse," *Politico*, February 27, 2022.

Michael Birnbaum, Missy Ryan, and Souad Mekhennet, "In Just 72 hours, Europe Overhauled Its Entire Post-Cold War Relationship with Russia," *Washington Post*, February 28, 2022.

George Packer, "Ukraine Is Redefining America's Interests," Atlantic, February 28, 2022.

Maura Reynolds, "'Yes, He Would': Fiona Hill on Putin and Nukes, Putin Is Trying to Take Down the Entire World Order, the Veteran Russia Watcher Said in an Interview. But There Are Ways Even Ordinary Americans Can Fight Back," *Politico*, February 28, 2022.

Kori Schake, "Putin Accidentally Revitalized the West's Liberal Order," *Atlantic*, February 28, 2022.

Richard Fontaine, "The Long Weekend That Changed History, Vladimir Putin's Invasion of Ukraine Means that the Post–Cold War Era May Have Just Ended," *Atlantic*, March 1, 2022.

Mary Elise Sarotte, "I'm a Cold War Historian. We're in a Frightening New Era," *New York Times*, March 1, 2022.

Martin Wolf, "Putin Has Reignited the Conflict between Tyranny and Liberal Democracy," *Financial Times*, March 1, 2022.

Anne Applebaum, "The Impossible Suddenly Became Possible, When Russia Invaded Ukraine, the West's Assumptions about the World Became Unsustainable," *Atlantic*, March 1, 2022.

Marc Fisher, "In One Week of War, Russia's Invasion of Ukraine May Have Veered History in a New Direction," *Washington Post*, March 2, 2022.

Iliya Kusa, "Why Putin's War on Ukraine Will Change Everything," *Focus Ukraine (Wilson Center)*, March 2, 2022.

Peter Martin and Jennifer Jacobs, "Improved Russia-China Ties Have Ominous Implications for the U.S.," *Bloomberg*, March 2, 2022.

Dan McKivergan, "China, Russia, and the Challenge Ahead, Xi Might Distance China from Putin's War Crimes, but It's Unlikely He'll Make a Strategic Break with Putin's Regime," *Dispatch*, March 2, 2022.

Elliott Abrams, "The New Cold War," *National Review*, March 3, 2022.

Aljazeera Centre for Studies, "The End of the Post-Cold War Era: Russia's Adventure in Ukraine Reshapes the Entire World Order," Aljazeera Centre for Studies, March 3, 2022.

Damir Marusic, "A New World Order," *Washington Examiner*, March 3, 2022.

Mykola Kapitonenko, "Russia's Invasion of Ukraine Has Changed the World," *National Interest*, March 4, 2022.

Damien Cave, "The War in Ukraine Holds a Warning for the World Order," *New York Times*, March 4 (updated March 6), 2022.

Yun Sun, "China's Strategic Assessment of Russia: More Complicated than You Think," *War on the Rocks*, March 4, 2022.

Sean Illing, "How the War in Ukraine Could Change History, A Political Scientist on Why the Fate of the Global Political Order Hangs in the Balance," *Vox*, March 5, 2022.

Wallace Gregson, "Russia's War of 'Iron and Blood' in Ukraine Has Changed Everything," *19FortyFive*, March 6, 2022.

Shadi Hamid, "There Are Many Things Worse Than American Power, Blaming U.S. Hegemony for Global Problems Has Been Easy, but Putin's Invasion of Ukraine Offers a Preview of a Much More Dangerous World," *Atlantic*, March 6, 2022.

Robert D. Blackwill and Richard Fontaine, "Ukraine War Should Slow But Not Stop the U.S. Pivot to Asia," *Bloomberg*, March 8, 2022.

Seth J. Frantzman, "World Won't Be Able to Back Out of Russia Sanctions, The Ukraine Invasion Is a Turning Point Because, Like the Pandemic, It Is Accelerating Existing Breakdowns in the World Order," *Jerusalem Post*, March 8, 2022.

Bret Stephens, "New Rules for a New World," *New York Times*, March 8, 2022.

Raf Casert, "With Ukraine War, Europe's Geopolitical Map Is Moving Again," *Associated Press*, March 9, 2022.

Seth Cropsey, "Russia's Failure Is China's Gain, This Isn't Another Cold War. Due to Putin's Invasion of Ukraine, the World Has Become More Dangerous Than It's Been Since World War II," *Wall Street Journal*, March 9, 2022.

Byron Kaye and Eduardo Baptista, "Russia, China in 'Strategic Convergence'—Australian Intelligence," *Reuters*, March 9, 2022.

Robert Daly, "China and the United States: It's a Cold War, but Don't Panic," *Bulletin of the Atomic Scientists*, March 10, 2022.

Tom McTague, "For the West, the Worst Is Yet to Come, Perhaps the Ukraine Crisis Has Saved the West from Its Pettiness and Division. But the Bigger Picture Is Far More Depressing," *Atlantic*, March 10, 2022.

Fareed Zakaria, "Putin's Invasion of Ukraine Marks the Beginning of a Post-American Era," *Washington Post*, March 10, 2022.

Josh Hammer, "The End of the Unipolar Moment," *Newsweek*, March 11, 2022.

Atlantic Council, "UK Foreign Minister: Putin's Invasion of Ukraine Is a 'Paradigm Shift on the Scale of 9/11,'" *Atlantic Council*, March 12, 2022.

Ben Rhodes, "We Have Reached a Hinge of History, Out of the Righteous Rage of This Moment, Perhaps a New World Can Be Born," *Atlantic*, March 13, 2022.

Bret Stephens, "This Is How World War III Begins," *New York Times*, March 15, 2022.

Guy Faulconbridge, "Russia Says Post-1991 'Illusions' about the West Are Over," *Reuters*, March 18, 2022.

Jakub Grygiel, "Ukraine War Shows the 'Rules-Based International Order' Is a Myth, There Are No Global Threats or Standards, Only Regional Equilibria Requiring Constant Maintenance," *Wall Street Journal*, March 28, 2022.

Sonya Seunghye Lim and Christopher Turner, "Did The Cold War Ever Really End?," *The Cipher Brief*, March 29, 2022.

Stephen M. Walt, "The Ukraine War Doesn't Change Everything, Russia's War Marks the Definitive End of America's Unipolar Moment and Returns the World to a State Best Explained by Realism," *Foreign Policy*, April 13, 2022.

Stephen Kotkin, "The Cold War Never Ended, Ukraine, the China Challenge, and the Revival of the West," *Foreign Affairs*, May/June 2022.

William R. Hawkins, "The Old World Order Endures," *Journal of Political Risk*, June 3, 2022.

John Paul Rathbone, "Russian Menace Brings Abrupt End to the West's 'Peace Dividend,'" *Financial Times*, June 7, 2022.

Citations from July 2022

David Rieff, "Can America Overcome a Century of Challenge?," *National Interest*, July 12, 2022.

Amin Saikal, "The West Is Facing a New Alliance of Autocracies and Theocracies," *Strategist (ASPI)*, July 12, 2022.

Harlan Ullman, "America's New Era of Dangerous Coexistence," *The Hill*, August 1, 2022.

Hal Brands, "Why Superpower Crises Are a Good Thing, A New Era Of Tensions Will Focus Minds And Break Logjams, As Cold War History Shows," *Foreign Policy*, August 5, 2022.

Matthew Kroenig, "International Relations Theory Suggests Great-Power War Is Coming, According to IR Textbooks, the United States, Russia, and China Are on a Collision Course," *Foreign Policy*, August 27, 2022.

Stephen Young, "The Age of Predatory Nuclear-Weapon States Has Arrived, Putin's Nuclear Threat Marks the Start of a New Era," *Politico*, September 20, 2022.

Brad DeLong, "The Long 20th Century Comes to a Shuddering End, An Era of Once-Undreamt-of Progress Is Over—And You Won't Like What Comes Next," *Foreign Policy*, October 2, 2022.

Marc Champion, Natalia Ojewska, Sudhi Ranjan Sen, and Natalia Drozdiak, "The Post-Cold War Era Is Gone. A New Arms Race Has Arrived," *Bloomberg*, February 17, 2023.

Andreas Kluth, "The Geopolitical Multiverse Is Back to Two Superpowers, China's Rise and Putin's Invasion of Ukraine Have Put a Stop to a Multipolar World Order," *Wall Street Journal*, February 22, 2022.

Appendix C. Articles on Grand Strategy and Geopolitics

This appendix presents citations to articles discussing grand strategy and geopolitics for the United States in a context of GPC.

Citations from 2012 through 2014

William C. Martel, "Why America Needs a Grand Strategy," *Diplomat*, June 18, 2012.

Aaron David Miller, "The Naiveté of Distance," *Foreign Policy*, March 31, 2014.

Robert Kaplan, "The Gift of American Power," *Real Clear World*, May 15, 2014.

William C. Martel, "America's Grand Strategy Disaster," *The National Interest*, June 9, 2014.

Adam Garfinkle, "The Silent Death of American Grand Strategy," *American Review*, 2014.

Christopher A. Ford, "Ending the Strategic Holiday: U.S. Grand Strategy and a 'Rising' China," *Asia Policy*, Number 18 (July 2014): 181-189.

William Ruger, "A Realist's Guide to Grand Strategy," *The American Conservative*, August 26, 2014.

Barry R. Posen, *Restraint: A New Foundation for U.S. Grand Strategy*, Cornell University Press, 2014, 256 pp. (Cornell Studies in Security Affairs).

R. D. Hooker, *The Grand Strategy of the United States*, Washington, National Defense University Press, October 2014, 35 pp. (INSS Strategic Monograph, Institute for National Strategic Studies).

F.G. Hoffman, "Grand Strategy: The Fundamental Considerations," *Orbis*, Volume 58, Issue 4 (Fall 2014), 2014: 472–485.

Michael Page, "Is 'Restraint' a Realistic Grand Strategy?" *Cicero Magazine*, October 21, 2014.

Bryan McGrath, "Unconstrained Grand Strategy," *War on the Rocks*, October 28, 2014.

Joseph Sarkisian, "American Grand Strategy or Grand Illusion?" *Cicero*, December 1, 2014.

Citations from January through June 2015

Chris Miller, "State of Disunion: America's Lack of Strategy is its Own Greatest Threat, *Cicero*, January 27, 2015.

Jerry Hendrix, *Avoiding Trivia: A Strategy for Sustainment and Fiscal Responsibility*, CNAS, February 2015, 36 pp.

Jim Mattis, "A New American Grand Strategy," Hoover Institution, February 26, 2015.

Stewart Patrick and Isabella Bennett, "Geopolitics Is Back—and Global Governance Is Out," *The National Interest*, May 12, 2015.

Alfred McCoy, "The Geopolitics of American Global Decline," *Real Clear World*, June 8, 2015.

Steve LeVine, "How China Is Building the Biggest Commercial-Military Empire in History," *Defense One*, June 9, 2015.

Thomas Vien, "The Grand Design of China's New Trade Routes," *Stratfor*, June 24, 2015.

Citations from July through December 2015

John R. Deni, "General Dunford Is Right About Russia, But Not Because of Their Nukes," *War on the Rocks*, July 13, 2015.

Frederick W. Kagan and Kimberly Kagan, "Putin Ushers in a New Era of Global Geopolitics," *AEI Warning Intelligence Update*, September 27, 2015.

Gideon Rachman, "A Global Test of American Power," *Financial Times*, October 12, 2015.

Joschka Fischer, "The Return of Geopolitics to Europe," *Project Syndicate*, November 2, 2015.

Marian Leighton, "Go South, Young Russian," *Weekly Standard*, December 28, 2015.

Citations from January through June 2016

John E. McLaughlin, "US Strategy and Strategic Culture from 2017," *Global Brief*, February 19, 2016.

Michael Auslin, "Asia's Mediterranean: Strategy, Geopolitics, and Risk in the Seas of the Indo-Pacific," *War on the Rocks*, February 29, 2016.

Eliot Cohen, Eric S. Edelman, and Brian Hook, "Presidential Priority: Restore American Leadership, *World Affairs*, Spring 2016.

H.R. McMaster, "Probing for Weakness," *Wall Street Journal*, March 23, 2016.

Parag Khanna, "The Brilliance of China's Grand Strategy: Don't 'Own' Land, Just 'Use' It," *The National Interest*, April 11, 2016.

Seth Cropsey, "New American Grand Strategy," *Real Clear Defense*, April 13, 2016.

Zbigniew Brzezinski, "Toward a Global Realignment," *The American Interest*, April 17, 2016.

Michael Mandelbaum, "America in a New World," *The American Interest*, May 23, 2016.

Robert D. Blackwell, "China's Strategy for Asia: Maximize Power, Replace America," *National Interest*, May 26, 2016.

John J. Mearsheimer and Stephen M. Walt, "The Case for Offshore Balancing," *Foreign Affairs*, June 13, 2016.

Stephen Sestanovich, "Do Americans Want a New 'Grand Strategy' or Less Overseas Engagement?" *Wall Street Journal*, June 16, 2016.

Denny Roy, "A More-Selective US Grand Strategy," *PacNet #53 (Pacific Forum CSIS)*, June 29, 2016.

Citations from July through September 2016

Frank G. Hoffman, "Retreating Ashore: The Flaws of Offshore Balancing," Foreign Policy Research Institute, July 5, 2017.

James Holmes, "Why Offshore Balancing Won't Work,: *National Interest*, July 18, 2016.

Schuyler Foerster and Ray Raymond, "Balanced Internationalism: 5 Core Principles to Guide U.S. National Security Policy," *National Interest*, July 31, 2016.

Robert D. Kaplan, "Is Primacy Overrated?" *National Interest*, August 7, 2016.

Barry R. Posen, "The High Costs and Limited Benefits of America's Alliances," *National Interest*, August 7, 2016.

Christopher Preble, Emma Ashford, and Travis Evans, "Let's Talk about America's Strategic Choices," *War on the Rocks*, August 8, 2016.

Ted Galen Carpenter and Eric Gomez, "East Asia and a Strategy of Restraint," *War on the Rocks*, August 10, 2016.

Michael Lind, "Can America Share Its Superpower Status?" *National Interest*, August 21, 2016.

Doug Bandow, "Why Washington Is Addicted to Perpetual War," *National Interest*, August 28, 2016.

Andrew J. Bacevich, "Ending Endless War," *Foreign Affairs*, September/October 2016.

Frank Hoffman, "The Consistent Incoherence of Grand Strategy," *War on the Rocks*, September 1, 2016.

Gregory R. Copley, "The Era of Strategic Containment is Over," *Defense & Foreign Affairs*, September 7, 2016.

Barry F. Lowenkron and Mitchell B. Reiss, "Pragmatic Primacy: How America Can Move Forward in a Changing World," *National Interest*, September 11, 2016.

William Ruger, "The Myth of American Retreat," *American Conservative*, September 13, 2016.

Christopher Preble, "New Rules for U.S. Military Intervention," *War on the Rocks*, September 20, 2016.

Anders Fogh Rasmussen, "Free Nations of the World, Unite!" *National Review*, September 22, 2016.

Citations from October through December 2016

Michael J. Mazarr, "The World Has Passed the Old Grand Strategies By," *War on the Rocks*, October 5, 2016.

Max Fisher and Amanda Taub, "Syria Provokes an American Anxiety: Is U.S. Power Really So Special?" *New York Times*, October 8, 2016.

Uri Friedman, "Donald Trump and the Coming Test of International Order," *Atlantic*, November 9, 2016.

Robert Kagan, "Trump Marks the End of America As World's 'Indispensable Nation,'" *Financial Times*, November 19, 2016.

Hugh White, "What's So Great About American World Leadership?" *Atlantic*, November 23, 2016.

Peter Feaver, "A Grand Strategy Challenge Awaits Trump," *Foreign Policy*, November 29, 2016.

Hal Brands and Peter Feaver, "Stress-Testing American Grand Strategy," *Survival*, vol. 58, 2016, Issue 6: 93-120 (published online November 21, 2016) (see also Hal Brands and Peter Feaver, "Stress-Testing the Foundations of American Grand Strategy," *War on the Rocks*, December 13, 2016).

Christopher A. Preble, "Should the United States Wage War for Friends?" *National Interest*, December 15, 2016.

Citations from January through June 2017

Andrew F. Krepinevich, *Preserving the Balance, A U.S. Eurasia Defense Strategy*, Center for Strategic and Budgetary Assessments, 2017, 117 pp.

Hal Brands et al., *Critical Assumptions and American Grand Strategy*, Center for Strategic and Budgetary Assessments, 2017, 57 pp.

Kori Schake, "Will Washington Abandon the Order?" *Foreign Affairs*, January/February 2017: 41-46.

Robert D. Kaplan, "Why Trump Can't Disengage America From the World," *New York Times*, January 6, 2017.

Frank Hoffman, "The Case for Strategic Discipline During the Next Presidency," *War on the Rocks*, January 10, 2017.

Robert "Jake" Bebber and Richard J. Harknett, "Thoughts on Grand Strategy," *The Navalist*, January 12, 2017.

Colin Kahl and Hal Brands, "Trump's Grand Strategic Train Wreck," *Foreign Policy*, January 31, 2017.

Robert Kaplan, "America Is a Maritime Nation," *Real Clear Defense*, January 24, 2017.

Robert Kagan, "Backing Into World War III," *Foreign Policy*, February 6, 2017.

David H. Petraeus, "America Must Stand Tall," *Politico Magazine*, February 6, 2017.

Randall L. Schweller, "A Third-Image Explanation for Why Trump Now: A Response to Robert Jervis's 'President Trump and IR Theory,'" *ISSF Policy Series*, February 8, 2017.

Stephen M. Walt, "The Donald versus 'The Blob,'" *ISSF Policy Series*, February 14, 2017.

Ash Jain et al., *Strategy of "Constrainment:" Countering Russia's Challenge to the Democratic Order*, Atlantic Council, March 2017, 23 pp.

Robert C. Rubel, "Exporting Security: China, the United States, and the Innovator's Dilemma," *Naval War College Review*, Spring 2017, pp. 11-28.

Paul Miller, "Reassessing Obama's Legacy of Restraint," *War on the Rocks*, March 6, 2017.

Mercy A. Kuo, "Statecraft and Grand Strategy: Assessing the US and China," *Diplomat*, March 31, 2017.

Patrick Cronin, "Maritime Power and U.S. Strategic Influence in Asia," *War on the Rocks*, April 11, 2017.

Hal Brands, "America's Allies Are in Decline. Here's How the US Should Adjust," *Defense One*, May 5, 2017.

Robert D. Kaplan, "The Return of Marco Polo's World and the U.S. Military Response," CNAS, undated but posted ca. May 12, 2017.

Jane Perlez and Yufan Huang, "Behind China's $1 Trillion Plan to Shake Up the Economic Order," *New York Times*, May 13, 2017.

Jane Perlez and Keith Bradsher, "Xi Jinping Positions China at Center of New Economic Order," *New York Times*, May 14, 2017.

Citations from July 2017 through December 2017

Prince Michael of Liechtenstein, "Opinion: Control of Trade Routes Is Decisive," Geopolitical Intelligence Services, July 21, 2017.

Andrew Beddow, "America Cannot Become a Global Rome," *National Interest*, July 25, 2017.

Enea Gjoza, "America Historically Had a Restrained Foreign Policy: It's Time to Return to It," *National Interest*, July 25, 2017.

Leon Hadar, "Why Washington's Global Strategy Failed," *National Interest*, July 30, 2017.

Harvey M. Sapolsky, "America's Endless Search for a Strategy," *National Interest*, August 4, 2017.

David Haas and Jack McKechnie, "U.S. Peacetime Strategy with China," EastWest Institute, August 11, 2017.

Robert D. Kaplan, "America's Darwinian Nationalism," *National Interest*, August 13, 2017.

Andrew A. Michta, "The West Needs a Strategy," *American Interest*, August 25, 2017.

Nina Silove, "Beyond the Buzzword: The Three Meanings of 'Grand Strategy,'" *Security Studies*, Vol. 27, No. 1, 2018. (Published online August 28, 2017.)

Auston Long, Linda Robinson, and Seth G. Jones, "Managing Chaos in an Era of Great Power Competition," *War on the Rocks*, September 5, 2017.

Daniel Kliman, "Wanted: A U.S. Strategic Response to China's Belt and Road Initiative," *National Interest*, September 7, 2017.

James Jay Carafano, *America Desperately Needs a New Grand Strategy for its Role in the World*, Heritage Foundation, September 11, 2017.

Thorsten Benner, "An Era of Authoritarian Influence? How Democracies Should Respond," *Foreign Affairs*, September 15, 2017.

Dean Cheng, *Confronting the Eurasian Powers of Russia and China*, Heritage Foundation, September 28, 2017.

Matthew Kroenig and Miyeon Oh, *A Strategy for the Trans-Pacific Century: Final Report of the Atlantic Council's Asia-Pacific Strategy Task Force*, Atlantic Council, October 2017, 58 pp. (Atlantic Council Strategy Paper No. 12.)

Gal Luft, *Silk Road 2.0: US Strategy toward China's Belt and Road Initiative*, Atlantic Council, October 2017, 59 pp. (Atlantic Council Strategy Paper No. 11.)

Mercy A. Kuo, "US Leadership in Asia and the Future of Geopolitics, Insights from Jamie Fly," *Diplomat*, October 11, 2017.

David Santoro, "Collective Security Is America's Only Hope," *National Interest*, October 15, 2017.

C. Raja Mohan, "The Confluence of Two Seas," *Indian Express*, October 26, 2017.

Ionut Popescu, "Grand Strategy Is Overrated," *Foreign Policy*, December 11, 2017.

Citations from January 2018 through June 2018

Francis P. Sempa, "Needed: A National Security Strategy Rooted in Geopolitics," *Real Clear Defense*, January 9, 2018.

Benn Steil, "How to Win a Great-Power Competition," *Foreign Affairs*, February 9, 2018.

Alasdair Roberts, "Grand Strategy Isn't Grand Enough," *Foreign Policy*, February 20, 2018.

Francis P. Sempa, "Mackinder's Century," *Real Clear Defense*, March 2, 2018.

Jennifer Loy, "Mackinder and Mahan: The Chinese Geopolitics in South Asia," *Real Clear Defense*, March 15, 2018.

Ionut Popescu, "Trump Doesn't Need a Grand Strategy," *Foreign Affairs*, May 21, 2018.

Thomas P. Cavanna, "What Does China's Belt and Road Initiative Mean for US Grand Strategy?" *Diplomat*, June 5, 2018.

Citations from July 2018 through December 2019

John Schuessler, "Making Grand Strategy Grand Again," *National Interest*, July 25, 2018.

Paul C. Avey, Jonathan N. Markowitz, Robert J. Reardon, "Disentangling Grand Strategy: International Relations Theory and U.S. Grand Strategy," *Texas National Security Review*, November 2018.

Andrew Erickson, "Make China Great Again: Xi's Truly Grand Strategy," *War on the Rocks*, October 30, 2019.

Citations from January 2020 through December 2020

Jasen J. Castillo, "Don't Leave Grand Strategy to the Generals," *National Interest*, October 31, 2019.

Elizabeth Cobbs and Kimberly C. Field, "Why Did the U.S. Kill Suleimani? The Attack Illustrates America's Lack of a Clear Grand Strategy—and Why We Need One Immediately," *New York Times*, January 7, 2020.

Amy Zegart, "The Race for Big Ideas Is On, The United States Faces Genuinely New Global Challenges—But Tries to Understand Them Using Outmoded Theories from a Bygone Era," *Atlantic*, January 13, 2020.

John T. Kuehn, "Revisiting Grand Strategy," *Journal of Political Risk*, May 2020.

Daniel W. Drezner, Ronald R. Krebs, and Randall Schweller, "The End of Grand Strategy, America Must Think Small," *Foreign Affairs*, May/June 2020.

James Holmes, "Is U.S. Grand Strategy Dead Thanks to Donald Trump?" *National Interest*, May 16, 2020.

Andrew Ehrhardt and Maeve Ryan, "Grand Strategy Is No Silver Bullet, But It Is Indispensable," *War on the Rocks*, May 19, 2020.

David H. McCormick, Charles E. Luftig, and James M. Cunningham, "Economic Might, National Security, and the Future of American Statecraft," *Texas National Security Review*, Summer 2020.

Anthony H. Cordesman, "Ending America's Grand Strategic Failures," CSIS, June 22, 2020.

Ryan Dukeman, "Can Congressional Diplomacy Work for Grand Strategy?" LegBranch.org, June 25, 2020.

Adam Yang, "A US Vision Beyond Great Power Competition," *East Asia Forum*, July 22, 2020.

Frank Hoffman, "Distilling the Essence of Strategy," *War on the Rocks*, August 4, 2020.

Micah Zenko and Rebecca Lissner, "This Is What America Looks Like Without Grand Strategy," *Foreign Policy*, August 18, 2020.

Rodger Baker, "China, the U.S., and the Geography of the 21st Century," *Stratfor*, August 21, 2020.

Francis J. Gavin, "Blame It on the Blob? How to Evaluate American Grand Strategy," *War on the Rocks*, August 21, 2020.

Zachary Tyson Brown, "The United States Needs a New Strategic Mindset," *Foreign Policy*, September 22, 2020.

Stephen M. Walt, "Is the Blob Really Blameless? How Not to Evaluate American Grand Strategy," *Foreign Policy*, September 22, 2020.

Ionut Popescu, "It's Too Soon For America To Kill Its Grand Strategy," *National Interest*, September 22, 2020.

Michael Shurkin, "Grand Strategy Is Total: French Gen. André Beaufre on War in the Nuclear Age," *War on the Rocks*, October 8, 2020.

Robert D. Kaplan, "The Afterlife of Empire," *National Interest*, October 16, 2020.

Luke Nicastro, "To Fix U.S. Foreign Policy, Look to the Balance of Power," *Real Clear Defense*, October 14, 2020.

George Beebe, "Balancing Great Power Politics in 2021 and Beyond," *National Interest*, October 17, 2020.

Michael Lind, "Thanks to China's Rise, the Age of Dealignment Is Here," *National Interest*, October 17, 2020.

James A. Winnefeld, Michael J. Morell, and Graham Allison, "Why American Strategy Fails, Ending the Chronic Imbalance Between Ends and Means," *Foreign Affairs*, October 28, 2020.

Bradley Bowman and Shane Praiswater, "Great Power Competition Comes Home to America," *Defense One*, November 3, 2020.

Austin Doehler, "Great Power Competition Is Too Narrow a Frame," *Defense One*, December 6, 2020.

Citations from January 2021 through June 2021

Mark F. Cancian, *Inflicting Surprise, Gaining Competitive Advantage in Great Power Conflicts*, CSIS, January 2021, 112 pp.

Erica D. Borghard, "A Grand Strategy Based on Resilience," *War on the Rocks*, January 4, 2021.

Francis P. Sempa, "Is China the 21st Century's Great 'Going Concern'? Halford Mackinder Is Famous for His 'Heartland' Theory, but Another of His Major Theoretical Constructs May Be More Relevant to China's Rise," *Diplomat*, January 5, 2021.

Kevin Bilms, "Avoid 'Great-Power Competition' in Future Security Strategies, Let's Ditch 'Great-Power Competition,' Call the Framing Idea 'Strategic Competition'—As It Is Referred to by the NDS—and Unpack the Implications of the Term," *National Interest*, January 6, 2021.

Clementine Starling and Matthew R. Crouch, "America's Next National Defense Strategy: Regaining the Advantage is the Name of the Game," *National Interest*, February 3, 2021.

Daniel H. Nexon, "Against Great Power Competition, The U.S. Should Not Confuse Means for Ends," *Foreign Affairs*, February 15, 2021.

Robert Farley, "Welcome to the All-Consuming Great Power Competition, The Rhetoric of Great Power Competition Threatens to Devour Every Other Aspect of U.S. Foreign Policy," *Diplomat*, February 23, 2021.

C. Anthony Pfaff, "'Great Power Competition' Is a Dangerously Simple Frame," *Defense One*, February 24, 2021.

Robert A. Manning and Peter A. Wilson, "Offshore Balancing Strategy Can Correct America's Middle East Approach," *National Interest*, February 26, 2021.

Zack Cooper and Hal Brands, "America Will Only Win When China's Regime Fails, There Are Two Possible Outcomes of U.S.-China Competition—But Washington Should Prepare for the More Turbulent One," *Foreign Policy*, March 11, 2021.

Mathew Burrows and Robert Manning, "Humility in American Grand Strategy," *War on the Rocks*, March 17, 2021.

James Traub, "Biden's 'Foreign Policy for the Middle Class' Is a Revolution, The New Administration Is Trying to Forge a New National Consensus on Grand Strategy That Doesn't Privilege the Rich," *Foreign Policy*, March 17, 2021.

Elbridge Colby, "Biden's Global, Muscular Liberalism Is an Indefensible Foreign Policy in 2021," *Washington Post*, March 21, 2021.

Hal Brands and Charles Edel, "A Grand Strategy of Democratic Solidarity," *Washington Quarterly*, Spring 2021: 29-47. (Published online March 23, 2021.)

Daniel W. Drezner, "If there is going to be a grand strategy focused on China ... Do Not Turn America's Greatest Strength into Its Greatest Weakness," *Washington Post*, March 23, 2021.

Robert A. Manning, "The U.S. Doesn't Need China's Collapse to Win, A Misguided Theory of Great-Power Competition Will Only Lead to Grief," *Foreign Policy*, March 24, 2021.

Leon Hadar, "Status Quo Joe: Why Biden's Grand Strategy Is MIA, Unfortunately, Much of What Happens in the Foreign-Policy Arena under U.S. Presidents, Including Important Decisions, Amounts to Ad Hoc Responses to Outside Events at Home and Abroad," *National Interest*, March 26, 2021.

Michael Beckley and Hal Brands, "America Needs to Rediscover Strategic MacGyverism, The United States Has Typically Relied on Strategic MacGyverism in Cases Where Novel Problems Spurred Fresh, High-Level Thinking While Creating Fierce Operational Urgency," *National Interest*, March 27, 2021.

Emma Ashford, "Great-Power Competition Is a Recipe for Disaster, The Latest Poorly Defined Buzzword in Washington Is Leading Pundits and Policymakers Down a Dangerous Path," *Foreign Policy*, April 1, 2021.

Daniel DePetris, "Don't Divide the World Between Democracies and Autocracies," *Defense One*, April 1, 2021.

Octavian Manea, "The West Needs to Redevelop the Tools and Mindset of Strategic Competition," *Small Wars Journal*, April 5, 2021. (Interview with Dr. A. Wess Mitchell.)

Stephen M. Walt, "What Comes After the Forever Wars, An Era of U.S. Grand Strategy Is Now Ending. Here's What Should Come Next," *Foreign Policy*, April 28, 2021.

Citations from July 2021 through December 2021

James Stavridis, "Great Power Competition Requires Theater Deterrence," *U.S. Naval Institute Proceedings*, July 2021.

Robert L. Wilkie, "America Needs a Grand Strategy," Heritage Foundation, July 23, 2021.

Michael J. Mazarr, "Time for a New Approach to Defense Strategy," *War on the Rocks*, July 29, 2021.

Joseph S. Nye, "America Needs a New Great-Power Strategy," *Strategist (ASPI)*, August 4, 2021.

Anna Simons, "Finessing Primacy—Some Military Considerations Before Subversion Does Us In, Part One," *Small Wars Journal*, August 11, 2021; and Anna Simons, "Finessing Primacy—Some Military Considerations Before Subversion Does Us In, Part Two," *Small Wars Journal*, August 11, 2021.

A. Wess Mitchell, "A Strategy for Avoiding Two-Front War," *National Interest*, August 22, 2021.

Heritage Foundation, "Freedom's Global Force Posture: A Grand Strategy For The 21st Century," *19FortyFive*, September 2, 2021.

Wyatt Olson, "'Strategic Distraction': 9/11 Took America's Eye off Asia as China Hit Its Military Stride," *Stars and Stripes*, September 9, 2021.

James Jay Carafano, "Getting a Game Plan for the Guardian of America's Global Interests, If the United States Can't Prevent China from Dominating Asia, Then the United States Loses," *National Interest*, September 12, 2021.

Robert L. Wilkie, *America Needs a Grand Strategy*, Heritage Foundation, November 3, 2021, 8 pp.

David T. Pyne, "To Counter Russia and China, Make 'Spheres of Influence' Great Again," *National Interest*, October 11, 2021.

Walter Russell Mead, "The Campaign to Distract Biden From Asia, China and Russia Form an Entente to Hobble America, with a Little Help from Iran," *Wall Street Journal*, November 22, 2021.

Hal Brands, "Containment Can Work Against China, Too, There Are Important Differences between Xi Jinping's China and the Soviet Union, but the Cold War Still Offers Clear Strategic Guidance for the U.S.," *Wall Street Journal*, December 3, 2021.

Daniel DePetris, "Hedging US Strategy Against an Emerging China-Russia Partnership," *Defense News*, December 22, 2021.

Arnel P. David, Sean A. Acosta, and Nicholas Krohley, "Getting Competition Wrong: The US Military's Looming Failure," *Modern War Institute*, December 3, 2021.

Citations from January 2022 through June 2022

Miranda Priebe, Kristen Gunness, Karl P. Mueller, and Zachary Burdette, *The Limits of Restraint, The Military Implications of a Restrained U.S. Grand Strategy in the Asia-Pacific*, RAND, 2022, 117 pp.

Daniel Blumenthal, "Beijing's Grand Strategy: A Sino-centric Order," Jewish Policy Center, Winter 2021 (posted online January 4, 2022).

Andreas Kluth, "The West Is Right to Deny Russia a 'Sphere of Influence,' NATO, the U.S. and the EU Can't Just Hand Eastern Europe to Vladimir Putin as His Fief. It's Not Theirs to Give," *Bloomberg*, January 13, 2022.

James P. Farwell and Michael Miklaucic, "America Needs a New Grand Strategy to Navigate the 21st Century," *Defense News*, January 25, 2022.

Joshua Rovner, "How Long Can Biden Muddle Through on China?" *War on the Rocks*, January 26, 2022.

Stephen M. Walt, "America Has an Unhealthy Obsession With Credibility, There's No Reason U.S. Grand Strategy Should Be So Concerned With Its Own Reputation," *Foreign Policy*, January 29, 2022.

Stephen S Roach, "China's Triangulation Gambit," *Project Syndicate*, February 10, 2022.

Elbridge Colby and Oriana Skylar Mastro, "Ukraine Is a Distraction From Taiwan, Getting Bogged Down in Europe Will Impede the U.S.'s Ability to Compete with China in the Pacific," *Wall Street Journal*, February 13, 2022.

Tucker Hamilton, "Comparing Russian, Chinese, and U.S. Overstretch," *American Security Project*, February 14, 2022.

Walter Russell Mead, "'Asia First' Misses the Point, The U.S. Needs a Coherent Strategy for Both Security and Economic Policy," *Wall Street Journal*, February 14, 2022.

John Bolton, "Entente Multiplies the Threat From Russia and China, The Misguided Idea that the U.S. Needs to Ignore One to Focus on the Other Intensifies the Danger," *Wall Street Journal*, February 15, 2022.

Brahma Chellaney, "America Is Focusing on the Wrong Enemy," *Strategist (ASPI)*, February 15, 2022.

Anthony H. Cordesman with the assistance of Grace Hwang, *NATO and the Ukraine: Reshaping NATO to Meet the Russian and Chinese Challenge*, CSIS, February 16, 2022, 62 pp.

Michael J. Green, and Gabriel Scheinmann, "Even an 'Asia First' Strategy Needs to Deter Russia in Ukraine, There Is No Indo-Pacific Strategy Without U.S. Pushback Against Russia," *Foreign Policy*, February 17, 2022.

Barry Pavel, "Biden Should Shift US Troop Positions Worldwide, The Crisis in Europe Makes Clear that Biden's Team Should Rethink Their First National Defense Strategy, Quickly," *Defense One*, February 17, 2022.

Hal Brands, "U.S. Can't Let Russia Create a Sphere of Influence, The Ukraine Crisis Strikes at the Heart of a 200-Year-Old Pillar of American Foreign Policy," *Bloomberg*, February 18, 2022.

Michael Hirsh, "What Biden Can Learn From Nixon About China, Fifty Years Later, Washington May Be Reversing a Diplomatic Masterstroke by Driving Beijing and Moscow Together," *Foreign Policy*, February 18, 2022.

Matthew Kroenig, "Washington Must Prepare for War With Both Russia and China, Pivoting to Asia and Forgetting About Europe Isn't an Option," *Foreign Policy*, February 18, 2022.

Douglas E. Schoen, "The Risks and Implications of China and Russia's Unholy Alliance," *The Hill*, February 20, 2022.

Farah Stockman, "This Is the Russia-China Friendship That Nixon Feared," *New York Times*, February 20, 2022.

Edward Wong, "Bond Between China and Russia Alarms U.S. and Europe Amid Ukraine Crisis," *New York Times*, February 20, 2022.

Raphael S. Cohen, "The False Choice Between China and Russia," *The Hill*, February 21, 2022.

Robert Kagan, "What We Can Expect After Putin's Conquest of Ukraine," *Washington Post*, February 21, 2022.

Holman W. Jenkins Jr., "Containing Russia, Old School, The U.S. and Allies Have Lots of Pressure Points on Putin, beyond Sanctions," *Wall Street Journal*, February 22, 2022.

Frederick W. Kagan, "Putin Has Changed the World—and the US Must Adapt or Lose," *The Hill*, February 22, 2022.

Charles Lane, "Does the World Have Answers for the Questions Putin Has Raised?" *Washington Post*, February 22, 2022.

Henry Olsen, "Diplomacy Failed to Deter Russia. Now's the Time for a New Cold War," *Washington Post*, February 22, 2022.

David Von Drehle, "Putin Is Reading from Stalin's Playbook. Here's How the West Should Handle Him," *Washington Post*, February 22, 2022.

Kathrin Hille, "Ukraine Crisis Saddles Washington with Indo-Pacific Dilemma, Asia Allies Fear Biden Administration Will be Distracted from Newly Minted Regional Strategy," *Financial Times*, February 23, 2022.

Alina Polyakova and Daniel Fried, "Putin's Long Game in Ukraine, How the West Can Still Protect Kyiv," *Foreign Affairs*, February 23, 2022.

Michael D. Swaine and J. Stapleton Roy, "Don't Use the Ukraine Crisis to Inflate the China Threat," *National Interest*, February 23, 2022.

Russell A. Berman and Michael Auslin, "Opening Up Second Fronts in Great Power Conflict," *National Interest*, February 24, 2022.

Stephen Blank, "The West Needs Containment 2.0," *The Hill*, February 24, 2022.

Josh Rogin, "From His Prison Cell, Georgia's Former President Reminds the West How to Deal with Putin," *Washington Post*, February 24, 2022.

David L. Phillips, "Contending With the New Russian Empire," *National Interest*, February 25, 2022.

David E. Sanger, "Biden Targets Russia With Strategy of Containment, Updated for a New Era," *New York Times*, February 25, 2022.

Jeremy Shapiro, "Why the West's China Challenge Just Got a Lot Harder, China Remains an Enormous Problem, and Russia's Invasion of Ukraine Only Makes It Worse," *Politico*, February 27, 2022.

Tony Bertuca, "DOD official: New National Defense Strategy Will Keep China First, But Reflect New Reality with Russia," *Inside Defense*, February 28, 2022.

Michael J. Mazarr, *Understanding Competition, Great Power Rivalry in a Changing International Order—Concepts and Theories*, RAND, March 2022, 51 pp.

Ivo H. Daalder, "The Return of Containment, How the West Can Prevail Against the Kremlin," *Foreign Affairs*, March 1, 2022.

Robert M. Gates, "We Need a More Realistic Strategy for the Post-Cold War Era," *Washington Post*, March 3, 2022.

Nikolas K. Gvosdev, "Can America Adapt to the Multipolar Age? Can an Increasingly Ossified National Security System and Dysfunctional Domestic Politics Allow the United States to Evolve Its Position and Policies to Cope with a Changing International Order?" *National Interest*, March 6, 2022.

Eliot A. Cohen, "The Strategy That Can Defeat Putin, The U.S.-Led Coalition of Liberal-Democratic States Should Pursue Three Objectives," *Atlantic*, March 7, 2022.

Bradley Thayer, "Russia's War In Ukraine: A Balance Of Power Problem For America?" *19FortyFive*, March 7, 2022.

Scott McCann, "Russia's War in Ukraine Demands U.S. Self-Reflection, The Pursuit of Primacy Has Pushed the United States to Pursue Maximalist Objectives. That Grand Strategy Has Exacerbated Conflicts and Harmed U.S. Interests with Almost No Debate About Its Efficacy," *National Interest*, March 8, 2022.

Joshua Tallis, "Strategy of the Commons: Defending the International Order Where it is Most Vulnerable," Strategy Bridge, March 9, 2022.

Thomas Meaney, "Putin Wants a Clash of Civilizations. Is 'The West' Falling for It?" *New York Times*, March 11, 2022.

Michael Crowley and Edward Wong, "Ukraine War Ushers In 'New Era' for U.S. Abroad, President Biden Is Rethinking Relationships with Allies as Well as Rivals—Including China, Iran and Venezuela—to Counter President Vladimir V. Putin of Russia," *New York Times*, March 12, 2022.

Ali Wyne, "America's Top Competitor Is Not Russia Or China, But Itself, The United States Has an Opportunity to Overcome the Inertia that Has Long Tethered Its Pursuit of Strategic Clarity to the Maneuvers of External Competitors," *National Interest*, March 12, 2022.

Michael Beckley and Hal Brands, "The Return of Pax Americana? Putin's War Is Fortifying the Democratic Alliance," *Foreign Affairs*, March 14, 2022.

A. Wess Mitchell, "To Prevent China from Grabbing Taiwan, Stop Russia in Ukraine," *National Interest*, March 14, 2022.

Seth Cropsey, "Russia-Ukraine War: US Must Change Its Role in Europe's Defense," *The Hill*, March 15, 2022.

Michael Barone, "Ukraine Points to the Dangers of the Eurasian Heartland Axis," *Washington Examiner*, March 16, 2022.

Aamer Madhani and Chris Megerian, "Biden's China 'Pivot' Complicated by Russia's War in Ukraine," *Associated Press*, March 17, 2022.

Michael W. Johnson, "After Russia's Ukraine Invasion, 7 Assumptions the US and NATO Allies Should Drop," *Breaking Defense*, March 18, 2022.

Gordon Lubold, David S. Cloud, and Lindsay Wise, "Ukraine War Complicates Biden Administration's Military Strategy on China and Russia, Russia's Invasion Is Forcing the Administration to Rethink Its Priorities, But It Still Sees Beijing as the Long-Term Threat," *Wall Street Journal*, March 21, 2022.

Anne-Marie Slaughter, Kishore Mahbubani, Stephen M. Walt, Toshihiro Nakayama, Shannon K. O'Neil, C. Raja Mohan, Robin Niblett, and Stefan Theil, "U.S. Grand Strategy After Ukraine, Seven Thinkers Weigh In on How the War Will Shift U.S. Foreign Policy," *Foreign Policy*, March 21, 2022.

Reuel Marc Gerecht and Ray Takeyh, "The Folly of the 'Pivot to Asia,' China Is a Rising Challenge, But Neglecting Europe and the Middle East Won't Help America Confront It," *Wall Street Journal*, March 22, 2022.

Kelly A. Grieco and Alec Evans, "Biden Should Nudge Europeans to Lead NATO," *Defense News*, March 22, 2022.

Al Jazeera and news agencies, "Biden Says Asia-Pacific Region Still a Priority amid Ukraine War, Ukraine War Threatens 'Rules-Based Order' Globally, Including in Asia-Pacific Region, US President Tells Singapore PM," *Al Jazeera*, March 29, 2022.

Anna Applebaum, "There Is No Liberal World Order, Unless Democracies Defend Themselves, the Forces of Autocracy Will Destroy Them," *Atlantic*, March 31, 2022.

Tom McTague, "The West's World War II Moment, The Principal Strategic Threat to the Western World Has Shifted, Creating a Whole New Set of Problems," *Atlantic*, April 4, 2022.

Hal Brands, "Opposing China Means Defeating Russia, Moscow's War Isn't a Distraction. It's Part and Parcel of the Threat Posed by Beijing," *Foreign Policy*, April 5, 2022.

Mary Brooks, "How to Focus on the China Challenge in the Midst of a Russian War," *National Interest*, April 6, 2022.

Charles A. Kupchan, "Putin's War in Ukraine Is a Watershed. Time for America to Get Real," *New York Times*, April 11, 2022.

Harlan Ullman, "Where Have All the Strategic Thinkers Gone?" *The Hill*, April 26, 2022.

Robert Kagan, "The Price of Hegemony, Can America Learn to Use Its Power?" *Foreign Affairs*, May/June 2022.

Arta Moeini and Coleman Hopkins, "America Needs Strategic Empathy in a Multipolar World, The Reality Is that Middle Powers Have Independent Security, Economic, and Regional Interests (Among Others) that Cut against America's Manichean Worldview and Abstract Objectives," *National Interest*, May 2, 2022.

Peter Martin, "Biden Team Sees China Tilt Aided as Putin Falters in Ukraine," *Bloomberg*, May 9, 2022.

Andrew Ehrhardt, "Recovering a Balance-of-Power Principle for the 21st Century," *War on the Rocks*, May 26, 2022.

Hal Brands, "The World Doesn't Need a More Restrained America, New Arguments for the US to Stop Involving Itself in Europe, the Middle East and Elsewhere Fail to Confront the Global Instability Such a Change Would Bring," *Bloomberg*, June 1, 2022.

Peter Martin and Jennifer Jacobs, "Putin's Invasion of Ukraine Forces Biden to Rewrite US Security Plan," *Bloomberg*, June 3, 2022.

Niall Ferguson, "Dust Off That Dirty Word Detente and Engage With China, Joe Biden's Grand Strategy Is Setting the US and Beijing on a Collision Course. It's Bad Foreign Policy and Terrible Domestic Politics," *Bloomberg*, June 5, 2022.

Nadège Rolland, "China's Southern Strategy, Beijing Is Using the Global South to Constrain America," *Foreign Affairs*, June 9, 2022.

Raphael BenLevi, "How Competing Schools of Grand Strategy Shape America's Nonproliferation Policy Toward Iran," *Texas National Security Review*, Summer 2022: 33-58.

Sascha Glaeser, "Asia Is More Important to the US Than Europe, and US Leaders Need to Start Acting Like It," *Business Insider*, June 23, 2022.

Citations from July 2022 through December 2022

Hal Brands, "The Art of the Arms Race, To Avoid Disaster, the United States Must Relearn Crucial Cold War Lessons," *Foreign Policy*, July 1, 2022.

Charles A. Kupchan, "How U.S. Strategy Can Succeed in a Multipolar Cold War, The West Now Needs to Downsize Its Idealist Ambitions, Realize that It Lives in a More Hobbesian World, and Pivot Back to a Grand Strategy Anchored by the Practice of Realpolitik," *National Interest*, July 3, 2022.

Joseph S. Nye Jr., "The War in Ukraine Exposed the Limits of 'Great Power Competition,' A Good Strategy Will Require the United States to Work with China at the Same Time that We Compete as Strategic Rivals," *National Interest*, July 3, 2022.

Edward Lucas, "The West Needs a Cure for Cold War Fever, Yes, a New Cold War Is Upon Us. It's Time to Stop Talking about It and Start Trying to Win It," *Foreign Policy*, July 5, 2022.

Sumantra Maitra, "Imperial Pressures: America Must Pass the Buck in Europe," *National Interest*, July 8, 2022.

Stephen M. Walt, "Biden Needs Architects, Not Mechanics, to Fix U.S. Foreign Policy, As the U.S. Midterms Near, Washington Is Plagued by Groupthink and a Lack of Vision that Prevents Creative Solutions to the Problems of a New Era," *Foreign Policy*, July 12, 2022.

Axel de Vernou, "No Pivot: The U.S. Can't Take on China Without Europe, By Splitting Its Attention between the Indo-Pacific and Europe, Washington Will Succeed in Focusing on Asia Without Leaving Anyone Behind," *National Interest*, July 18, 2022.

Nikolas K. Gvosdev, "The Regional Dimension to U.S. National Security," Foreign Policy Research Institute, July 20, 2022.

Garrett Martin, "No Narrative, No Support, No Problem: Crafting Grand Strategy in Postmodern America," *Small Wars Journal*, August 25, 2022.

George Beebe, *Managed Competition: A U.S. Grand Strategy for a Multipolar World*, Quincy Institute for Responsible Statecraft, Quincy Brief No. 30, September 2022, 14 pp.

Anders Fogh Rasmussen, Angela Stent, Stephen M. Walt, C. Raja Mohan, Robin Niblett, Liana Fix, and Edward Alden, "How U.S. Grand Strategy Is Changed by Ukraine," *Foreign Policy*, September 2, 2022. (Presents short essays by seven authors.)

Andrew Latham, "Spheres of Influence in a Multipolar World," *Defense Priorities*, September 26, 2022.

Colin Dueck, *Offshore Balancing, The British Analogy, 1688-1763*, American Enterprise Institute, October 2022, 42 pp.

Hal Brands, "America Can Contain China With an Alliance of Five, Conflict in the Indo-Pacific Looks Increasingly Plausible, and the US Is Going to Need Lots of Help from Australia, India, Japan and the UK," *Bloomberg*, November 2, 2022.

Bret Stephens, "Are We Sleepwalking Through a 'Decisive Decade'? *New York Times*, December 6, 2023.

Citations from January 2023

Frank Hoffman, "American Defense Priorities After Ukraine," *War on the Rocks*, January 2, 2023.

Jason Willick, "Why the U.S. Must Calculate a 'Solvency' Risk as It Arms Ukraine," *Washington Post*, January 19, 2023.

John R. Deni, "What Tanks in Ukraine Tell Us About America in the Pacific, U.S. Hopes that Europe Can Take Care of Itself Appear to Be Farfetched," *Defense One*, February 7, 2023.

Harlan Ullman, "The US Needs Strategic Replacements for Containment and Extended Deterrence," *The Hill*, March 6, 2023.

Fareed Zakaria, "America's Foreign Policy Has Lost All Flexibility," *Washington Post*, March 17, 2023.

David Ignatius, "Here's the real lesson from the showy Xi-Putin meeting," *Washington Post*, March 21, 2023.

Hal Brands, Peter D. Feaver, and William Inboden, "Stress Testing American Grand Strategy II: Critical Assumptions and Great-Power Rivalry," American Enterprise Institute, April 11, 2023.

Andrew A. Michta, "Ukraine Vs. Taiwan: America's Defeatist, Pointless Debate," *19FortyFive*, May 17, 2023.

Melanie W. Sisson, "The Biden Administration's Dangerous Grand Strategy, Can the Liberal International Order Survive the Strategy to Save It?" *Lawfare*, May 21, 2023.

Emma Ashford, Joshua R. Itzkowitz Shifrinson, Stephen Wertheim, and Michael J. Mazarr, "Does America Still Need Europe? Debating an 'Asia First' Approach," *Foreign Affairs*, May 22, 2023.

Stephen M. Walt, "Stop Worrying About Chinese Hegemony in Asia," *Foreign Policy*, May 31, 2023.

Hal Brands, "Ukraine's Survival Is Vital to Japan, South Korea and Taiwan," *Bloomberg*, June 1, 2023.

Suzanne Loftus, "America Cannot Compete with Russia and China for the Entirety of the Global South," *National Interest*, June 2, 2023.

Fareed Zakaria, "The United States Can No Longer Assume that the Rest of the World Is on Its Side," *Washington Post*, June 2, 2023.

Anne Pierce, "Authoritarian Cooperation Requires Elevated American Foreign Policy," *National Interest*, June 3, 2023.

Hal Brands, "The Battle for Eurasia: China, Russia, and Their Autocratic Friends Are Leading Another Epic Clash over the World's Largest Landmass," *Foreign Policy*, June 4, 2023.

Anthony H. Cordesman, *The Key Lessons of America's Recent Wars: Failing or Losing in Grand Strategic Terms*, Center for Strategic and International Studies (CSIS), June 13, 2023, 42 pp.

Daniel W. Drezner, "The Futility of Grand Strategy," *Foreign Policy*, June 18, 2023.

Niall Ferguson, "America Still Leads the World, But Its Allies Are Uneasy, In the Global Struggle between the Eurasian 'Heartland' and the US-led 'Rimland,' There's Trouble Ahead," *Bloomberg*, June 18, 2023.

Elliot M. Seckler and Travis Zahnow, *America's Reactive Foreign Policy: How U.S. Organizational Culture and Behavior Advantages China*, Andrew W. Marshall Foundation, July 2013, 25 pp.

Becca Wasser, *Campaign of Denial, Strengthening Simultaneous Deterrence in the Indo-Pacific and Europe*, Center for a New American Security (CNAS), August 2023, 56 pp.

Appendix D. Readings on Supply Chain Security

This appendix presents citations for further reading on the issue of supply chain security.

Executive Branch Documents and Documents Produced for the Executive Branch

Jon Boyens et al., *Supply Chain Risk Management Practices for Federal Information Systems and Organizations*, National Institute of Standards and Technology, NIST Special Publication 800-161, April 2015, 282 pp.

Defense Science Board, *[Report of] Task on Cyber Supply Chain*, February 2017, 69 pp.

National Defense Industrial Association, *Implementing Cybersecurity in DoD Supply Chains*, White Paper, July 2018, 17 pp.

Chris Nissen et al., *Deliver Uncompromised, A Strategy for Supply Chain Security and Resilience in Response to the Changing Character of War*, MITRE Corporation, August 2018, 55 pp.

Department of Defense, Inspector General, *Air Force Space Command Supply Chain Risk Management of Strategic Capabilities*, DODIG-2018-143, August 13, 2018, 36 pp.

Department of Defense, *Assessing and Strengthening the Manufacturing and Defense Industrial Base and Supply Chain Resiliency of the United States*, September 2018, 140 pp.

Defense Logistics Agency, *Supply Chain Security Strategy, Strengthening Operational Resiliency*, Appendix 1 to DLA's 2018-2026 Strategic Plan, undated (although the main part of DLA's strategic plan, as amended, is dated April 2019), 9 pp.

Memorandum from Michael D. Griffin, Under Secretary of Defense, Research and Engineering, for Chairman, Defense Science Board, Subject: Terms of Reference—Defense Science Board Task Force on 21st Century Industrial Base for National Defense, October 30, 2019.

Department of Defense, *Securing Defense-Critical Supply Chains, An Action Plan Developed in Response to President Biden's Executive Order 14017*, February 2022, 74 pp.

Congressional Report

House Armed Services Committee, *Report of the Defense Critical Supply Chain Task Force*, July 22, 2021, 23 pp.

GAO Reports

GAO has issued several reports over the years addressing supply chain issues, including supply chain security. Examples include the following:

Government Accountability Office, *Supply Chain Resilience[:] Agencies Are Taking Steps to Expand Diplomatic Engagement and Coordinate with International Partners*, GAO-23-105534, February 2023, 27 pp.

Government Accountability Office, *Defense Supplier Base[:] Challenges and Policy Considerations Regarding Offshoring and Foreign Investment Risks*, GAO-19-516, September 2019, 41 pp.

Government Accountability Office, *Nuclear Supply Chain: NNSA Should Notify Congress of Its Recommendations to Improve the Enhanced Procurement Authority*, GAO-19-606R, August 8, 2019, 11 pp.

Government Accountability Office, *Nuclear Supply Chain: DOE Has Not Used Its Enhanced Procurement Authority but Is Assessing Potential Use*, GAO-18-572R, August 2, 2018, 8 pp.

Government Accountability Office, *Information Security[:] Supply Chain Risks Affecting Federal Agencies*, Testimony before the Subcommittees on Counterterrorism and Intelligence, and Oversight and Management Efficiency, Committee on Homeland Security, House of Representatives, Statement of Gregory C. Wilshusen Director, Information Security Issues, GAO-18-667T, July 12, 2018, 12 pp.

Government Accountability Office, *Nuclear Supply Chain[:] DOE Should Assess Circumstances for Using Enhanced Procurement Authority to Manage Risk*, GAO-16-710, August 2016, 18 pp.

Government Accountability Office, *Rare Earth Materials[:] Developing a Comprehensive Approach Could Help DOD Better Manage National Security Risks in the Supply Chain*, GAO-16-161, February 2016, 34 pp.

Government Accountability Office, *Telecommunications Networks[:] Addressing Potential Security Risks of Foreign-Manufactured Equipment*, Testimony Before the Subcommittee on Communications and Technology, Committee on Energy and Commerce, House of Representatives, Statement of Mark L. Goldstein, Director Physical Infrastructure Issues, May 21, 2013, 49 pp.

Government Accountability Office, *IT Supply Chain[:] Additional Efforts Needed by National Security-Related Agencies to Address Risks*, GAO-12-579T, March 27, 2012 (Testimony Before the Subcommittee on Oversight and Investigations, Committee on Energy and Commerce, House of Representatives, Statement of Gregory C. Wilshusen, Director Information Security Issues), 10 pp.

Government Accountability Office, *IT Supply Chain[:] National Security-Related Agencies Need to Better Address Risks*, GAO-12-361, March 2012, 40 pp.

CRS Reports

Some examples of CRS reports discussing aspects of the issue include the following:

CRS In Focus IF10920, *Cyber Supply Chain Risk Management: An Introduction*, by Chris Jaikaran.

CRS In Focus IF11226, *Defense Primer: Acquiring Specialty Metals and Sensitive Materials*, coordinated by Heidi M. Peters.

CRS In Focus IF11259, *Trade Dispute with China and Rare Earth Elements*, by Karen M. Sutter.

CRS Report R41347, *Rare Earth Elements: The Global Supply Chain*, by Marc Humphries.

CRS Report R43864, *China's Mineral Industry and U.S. Access to Strategic and Critical Minerals: Issues for Congress*, by Marc Humphries.

CRS Report R45810, *Critical Minerals and U.S. Public Policy*, by Marc Humphries.

CRS Report R44544, *U.S. Semiconductor Manufacturing: Industry Trends, Global Competition, Federal Policy*, by Michaela D. Platzer and John F. Sargent Jr. (see the section entitled "National Security Concerns").

Press Reports and Other Readings

Michael Peck, "The U.S. Military's Greatest Weakness? China 'Builds' a Huge Chunk of It," *National Interest*, May 26, 2018.

Robert Metzger, "Federal Supply-Chain Threats Quietly Growing," *Federal Times*, August 13, 2018.

Peter Navarro, "America's Military-Industrial Base Is at Risk," *New York Times*, October 4, 2018.

Carla Babb and Hong Xie, "US Military Still Buying Chinese-Made Drones Despite Spying Concerns," *VOA News*, September 17, 2019.

Carla Babb, "US Military Still Buying Chinese-Made Drones Despite Spying Concerns," *VOA News*, September 17, 2019.

Peter Spiegel and Andrew Edgecliffe-Johnson, "US Navy Secretary Warns of 'Fragile' Supply China," *Financial Times*, November 5, 2019.

Nicole Hong, "A Military Camera Said 'Made in U.S.A. The Screen Was in Chinese," *New York Times*, November 7, 2019.

Scott Maucione, "Top DoD Scientist Sets Up Task Forces to Look at Industrial Base, Infrastructure," *Federal News Network*, November 25, 2019.

Lance Noble, "Defense Drives US Decoupling," Gavekal Dragonomics, January 13, 2020, 4 pp.

James Kynge and Mercedes Ruehl, "US-China Decoupling Hits Taiwan Chip Giant," *Financial Times*, January 15, 2020.

Asa Fitch, Kate O'Keeffe, and Bob Davis, "Trump and Chip Makers Including Intel Seek Semiconductor Self-Sufficiency," *Wall Street Journal*, May 11, 2020.

Thomas Ayres, "The US Needs to Rethink Its Overseas Supply Chain," *Defense News*, May 22, 2020.

Keith Johnson and Robbie Gramer, "U.S. Falters in Bid to Replace Chinese Rare Earths," *Foreign Policy*, May 25, 2020.

Adam A. Scher and Peter L. Levin, "Imported Chips Make America's Security Vulnerable," *Wall Street Journal*, May 25, 2020.

Matthew Beinart, "Lord Focused On Bolstering DoD's Domestic Supply Chain For Microelectronics, Rare Earth Mineral Processing," *Defense Daily*, July 8, 2020.

Justin Doubleday, "Pentagon Acquisition Chief Calls to 'Re-shore As Much As Possible' in Wake of COVID Supply Chain Challenges," *Inside Defense*, July 8, 2020.

Jacqueline Feldscher, "Pandemic's 'Silver Lining': A New Push to Build Equipment in the U.S.," *Politico Pro*, July 8, 2020.

"The Challenge of Reshoring the Defense Department Supply Chain," Govini, August 2020.

Jacob Helberg, "In the New Cold War, Deindustrialization Means Disarmament," *Foreign Policy*, August 12, 2020.

Rob Rosenberg, "Great Power Competition and Global Supply Chains," *The Hill*, August 19, 2020.

Jerry McGinn, "Reshoring Does Not Mean 'Buy America' Only," *Defense News*, September 15, 2020.

Paul McLeary, "Worried About Chinese Backdoors, Lord Pushes For New Tech Strategy," *Breaking Defense*, September 29, 2020.

Eli Nachmany, "Securing the Critical Minerals Supply Chain," *Lawfare*, October 21, 2020.

Justin Doubleday, "Pentagon Acquisition Chief Proposes 'Step-by-Step process' to Bring Microelectronics Back to U.S.," *Inside Defense*, November 10, 2020.

Ben Wolfgang, "'Reshore': U.S. Military's Reliance on China, Other Foreign Suppliers Exposed by Pandemic," *Washington Times*, December 10, 2020.

Sydney J. Freedberg Jr., "'Made In USA' Won't Secure Supply Chain Vs. China: Solarium," *Breaking Defense*, January 19, 2021.

Hiroyuki Suzuki, *Building Resilient Global Supply Chains, The Geopolitics of the Indo-Pacific Region*, CSIS, February 2021, 7 pp.

Justin Doubleday, "Pentagon Acquisition CISO: 2021 'The Year of Supply Chain Risk Management,'" *Inside Defense*, February 2, 2021.

Demetri Sevastopulo, "Biden to Order Review of Critical US Supply Chains," *Financial Times*, February 2, 2021.

Paul McLeary, "China Supply Chain, Backdoor Money 'Huge Priority' For Biden Pentagon," *Breaking Defense*, February 11, 2021.

Peggy Hollinger and Helen Warrell, "MPs Call for Ban on China and Russia Investing in UK Defence Supply Chain," *Financial Times*, February 13, 2021.

United Kingdom, House of Commons, Defense Committee, *Foreign Involvement in the Defence Supply Chain*, Fourth Report of Session 2019–21, HC 699, ordered to be printed February 9, 2021, published on February 14, 2021, 38 pp.

Aviation Week, "Halt Supply Chains Linked To China, UK Defense Committee Says," *Aviation Week*, February 15, 2021.

Sun Yu in Beijing and Demetri Sevastopulo, "China Targets Rare Earth Export Curbs to Hobble US Defence Industry, Beijing Asks Industry Executives If Proposed Restrictions Will Harm Western Contractors," Financial Times, February 16, 2021.

Theresa Hitchens, "US Industry Struggles To Strip Chinese Tech From Networks," *Breaking Defense*, February 22, 2021.

Taisei Hoyama and Yu Nakamura, "US and Allies to Build 'China-free' Tech Supply Chain," *Nikkei Asia*, February 24, 2021.

Demetri Sevastopulo and Aime Williams, "Joe Biden Orders Review of Critical Foreign Supply chains," *Financial Times*, February 24, 2021.

Megan Lamberth, Martijn Rasser, Ryan Johnson, and Henry Wu, *The Tangled Web We Wove, Rebalancing America's Supply Chains*, CNAS, March 2022, 30 pp.

Maiya Clark, "Biden's Supply Chain Executive Order Doesn't Boost the Defense Industrial Base—And That's OK, Joe Biden Has Wisely Opted Not to Start from Scratch But Instead to Build upon Donald Trump's Executive Order," *National Interest*, March 2, 2021.

Eric Onstad, "Five Eyes Alliance Urged to Forge Ties with Greenland to Secure Minerals," *Reuters*, March 4, 2021.

Justin Doubleday, "After 'Searing' COVID Shortfalls, House Lawmakers Eye Foreign Dependencies in Defense Supply Chain," *Inside Defense*, March 10, 2021.

Jane Nakano, *The Geopolitics of Critical Minerals Supply Chains*, CSIS, March 2021, 33 pp. (Posted March 11, 2021.)

Robert Morgus and John Costello, "What the Biden Administration Gets Right and Wrong on ICT in the New Supply Chain Executive Order," *Lawfare*, March 18, 2021. (ICT is information and communications technology.)

Paul McLeary, "DoD's New Pushback Against Chinese Money In US Defense Industry," *Breaking Defense*, April 12, 2021.

Chris Peters, "It's More Than Chips: Other Risks Exist in Defense Electronics Supply Chain," *C4ISRNet*, June 23, 2021.

Colin Clark, "HASC Task Force: Six Ways To Limit DoD's Dependence On Chinese Parts," *Breaking Defense*, July 22, 2021.

William R. Hawkins, "Supply Chains Must Adjust to Great Power Competition," *National Interest*, August 1, 2021.

Brad D. Williams, "Congressional Report Could Be Major Step To Strengthen US Defense Supply Chain," *Breaking Defense*, August 4, 2021.

Brad D. Williams, "DoD Forms New Task Force To Shore Up Supply Chain," *Breaking Defense*, September 7, 2021.

Jaspreet Gill, "DARPA Launches New Rare Earth Project to Reduce Reliance on China," *Inside Defense*, September 9, 2021.

Stephanie Halcrow, "Want To Solve Supply Chain Security? Do Business Differently, It's Time to Make Real Changes to the DFARS Requirements, Writes Stephanie Halcrow.," *Breaking Defense*, September 17, 2021.

Robert Dohner, "The United States Must Ensure Semiconductor Supply-Chain Resilience—Not Allocate Short Supplies," *Atlantic Council*, January 3, 2022.

Ellen Lord and Mira Ricardel, "America Needs a Robust, Resilient Supply Chain for Semiconductors," *Defense News*, February 11, 2022.

June Teufel Dreyer, "Rare Earths, Scarce Metals, and the Struggle for Supply Chain Security," Foreign Policy Research Institute, March 30, 2022.

Bryant Harris, "The US Is Heavily Reliant on China and Russia for Its Ammo Supply Chain. Congress Wants to Fix That," *Defense News*, June 8, 2022.

Elliot Ackerman, "The War in Ukraine Has Exposed a Critical American Vulnerability, Shoring Up the Nation's Supply Chain Is the Single Greatest Challenge to the National Defense," *Atlantic*, June 14, 2022.

Bryant Harris, "After Years of Inattention, Congress Scrambles to Save Defense Supply Chain," *Defense News*, July 26, 2022.

Maiya Clark, "Congress Should Use Targeted Restrictions—Not Domestic Content Requirements—to Protect Defense Supply Chains," *Heritage Foundation*, March 29, 2022.

Doug Cameron, "Pentagon Pushes Defense Companies to Limit Use of Chinese Supplies," *Wall Street Journal*, September 18, 2022.

AI-76

Tony Bertuca, "LaPlante Pushes 'Friend-Shoring' Ahead of Key Global Armaments Conference," *Inside Defense*, September 27, 2022.

Craig Hooper, "Embedding 'Proactive Vigilance' Into The Pentagon's High-Tech Supply Chain," *Forbes*, November 1, 2022.

Davis Winkie and Colin Demarest, "Official Army App Had Russian Code, Might Have Harvested User Data," *Army Times*, November 15, 2023.

James Pearson and Marisa Taylor, "Russian Software Disguised as American Finds Its Way into U.S. Army, CDC Apps," *Reuters*, November 16, 2023.

Richard Weitz, "Chipping Away at China's Semiconductor Threats to US Military, US Military Can't Rely on Chinese Semiconductors Because of Unreliable Supply Chain," *Fox News*, November 22, 2022.

"The 'Friend-Shoring' of Supply Chains," International Institute for Strategic Studies (IISS), December 2022.

Bradley Martin, et al., Supply Chain Interdependence and Geopolitical Vulnerability, The Case of Taiwan and High-End Semiconductors, RAND, 2023, 61 pp.

Thomas Ewing and James Byrne, "Supply Chains Are on the Geopolitical Front Lines: We're Not Ready," *The Hill*, January 3, 2023.

Sasha Romanosky, "Software Supply Chain Risk Is Growing, But Mitigation Solutions Exist," *The Hill*, January 24, 2023.

Justin Sherman, "Global Technology Products, U.S. Security Policy, and Spectrums of Risk," *Lawfare*, February 3, 2023.

Morgan D. Bazilian, Emily J. Holland, and Joshua Busby, "America's Military Depends on Minerals That China Controls, Rethinking Supply Chains Is Vital for U.S. Security," *Foreign Policy*, March 16, 2023.

Conor M. Savoy, *The Promise of Strategic Shoring, Supply Chain Resilience, Economic Growth, and Development Finance*, Center for Strategic and International Studies (CSIS), June 2023, 28 pp.

Appendix E. Articles on Russian and Chinese Irregular, Hybrid, and Gray-Zone Warfare

This appendix presents citations to articles discussing Russian and Chinese irregular, hybrid, and gray-zone warfare tactics and possible U.S. strategies for countering those tactics.

Citations from July through September 2015

Thomas Gibbons-Neff, "The 'New' Type of War That Finally Has The Pentagon's Attention," *Washington Post*, July 3, 2015.

Mark Galeotti, "Time to Think About 'Hybrid Defense,'" *War on the Rocks*, July 30, 2015.

A. Wess Mitchell, "The Case for Deterrence by Denial," *American Interest*, August 12, 2015.

Audrey Kurth Cronin, "The Changing Face Of War In The 21st Century," *Real Clear Defense*, August 18, 2015.

Aapo Cederberg and Pasi Eronen, "Wake Up, West! The Era of Hyrbid Warfare Is Upon Us," *Overt Action*, August 25, 2015.

Marcus Weisgerber, "Now NATO's Prepping for Hybrid War," *Defense One*, August 27, 2015.

Maria Snegovaya, *Putin's Information Warfare in Ukraine*, Washington, Institute for the Study of War, September 2015, 26 pp.

Citations from October through December 2015

Jan Joel Andersson and Thierry Tardy, *Hybrid: What's In a Name?*, European Union Institute for Security Studies, October 2015, 4 pp.

Megan Eckstein, "U.S. Naval Commander in Europe: NATO Needs to Adapt to Russia's New Way of Hybrid Warfare," *USNI News*, October 6, 2015.

Tony Wesolowsky and Mark Krutov, "Activist Says Russia Using 'Hybrid Warfare' in Syria," *Radio Free Europe/Radio Liberty*, November 11, 2015.

Howard Altman, "'Gray Zone Conflicts Far More Complex to Combat, Says Socom Chief Votel," *Tampa Tribune*, November 28, 2015 (updated November 29, 2015).

Jordan Chandler Hirsch and Peter Feaver, "Obama's Thin Gray Line," *Foreign Policy*, December 2, 2015.

Eric Olsen, "America's Not Ready for Today's Gray Wars," *Defense One*, December 10, 2015.

Adam Elkus, "50 Shades of Gray: Why Gray Wars Concept Lacks Strategic Sense," *War on the Rocks*, December 15, 2015.

Peter Pomerantsev, "Fighting While Friending: The Grey War Advantage of ISIS, Russia, and China," *Defense One*, December 29, 2015.

Citations from January through June 2016

David S. Maxwell, "Congress Has Embraced Unconventional Warfare: Will the US Military and The Rest of the US Government?" *Small Wars Journal*, December 29, 2016.

Joseph L. Votel et al., "Unconventional Warfare in the Gray Zone," *Joint Force Quarterly*, 1st Quarter 2016: 101-109.

Julian E. Barnes, "NATO Works to Adapt to More Ambiguous Warfare Techniques," *Wall Street Journal*, February 8, 2016.

Andreas Umland, *Russia's Pernicious Hybrid War Against Ukraine*, Atlantic Council, February 22, 2016.

Maxim Trudolyubov, "Russia's Hybrid War," *New York Times*, February 24, 2016.

Bret Perry, "How NATO Can Disrupt Russia's New Way of War," *Defense One*, March 3, 2016; Michael Kofman, "Russian Hybrid Warfare and Other Dark Arts," *War on the Rocks*, March 11, 2016.

Eerik-Niiles Kross, "Putin's War of Smoke and Mirrors," *Politico*, April 9, 2016.

Molly McKew, "Estonian Report Details Russia's 'Hybrid Threat' to Europe," *Washington Free Beacon*, April 18, 2016.

David Barno and Nora Bensahel, "A New Generation of Unrestricted Warfare," *War on the Rocks*, April 19, 2016.

Nathan Freier and Christopher Compton, "Gray Zone: Why We're Losing the New Era of National Security," *Defense One*, June 9, 2016.

Citations from July through December 2016

Dan Goure, "NATO vs. Russia: How to Counter the Hybrid Warfare Challenge," *National Interest*, July 7, 2016.

Dominik P. Jankowski, "Hybrid Warfare: A Known Unknown?" *Foreign Policy Blogs*, July 18, 2016.

Nicholas Fedyk, "Russian 'New Generation' Warfare: Theory, Practice, and Lessons for U.S. Strategists," *Small Wars Journal*, August 25, 2016.

Martin N. Murphy, *Understanding Russia's Concept for Total War in Europe*, Heritage Foundation, September 12, 2016.

Robert Caruso, "To Counter Russian Disinformation, Look to Cold War Tactics," *Defense One*, September 20, 2016.

Max Boot, "How to Wage Hybrid War on the Kremlin," *Foreign Policy*, December 13, 2016.

Citations from January through June 2017

Raine Tiessalo, "Finland Prepares for 'Manifold Warfare' as Russia Feeds Paranoia," *Bloomberg*, January 19, 2017.

Tim Mak, "U.S. Preps for Infowar on Russia," *Daily Beast*, February 6, 2017.

Joe Gould, "European Diplomats Urge Support for U.S. Soft Power Against Russia," *Defense News*, March 7, 2017.

Jakub Janda, *Six Immediate Steps to Stop Putin's Aggression*, Atlantic Council, March 13, 2017.

Jussi Rosendahl and Tuomas Forsell, "EU, NATO Countries Kick Off Center to Counter 'Hybrid' Threats," *Reuters*, April 11, 2017.

Jen Judson, "Countering 'Little Green Men': Pentagon Special Ops Studies Russia 'Gray Zone' Conflict," *Defense News*, May 15, 2017.

Peter Kreko and Lorant Gyori, *From Russia with Hate: The Kremlin's Support for Violent Extremism in Central Europe*, Atlantic Council, May 17, 2017.

Molly K. McKew, "Forget Comey: The Real Story Is Russia's War on America," *Politico*, June 11, 2017.

Ben Schreckinger, "How Russia Targets the U.S. Military," *Politico*, June 12, 2017.

Van Jackson, "Tactics of Strategic Competition," *Naval War College Review*, Summer 2017: 39-61.

James J. Wirtz, "Life in the 'Gray Zone': Observations for Contemporary Strategists," *Defense & Security Analysis*, vol. 33, no. 2, 2017: 106-114.

Citations from July 2017 through December 2017

Daniel Calingaert, "How Dictators Use Our Open Society Against Us," *The Hill*, July 6, 2017.

Christopher Walker, "A New Era of Competition, The Growing Threat from Authoritarian Internationalism as a Global Challenge to Democracy," *International Reports*, Issue 2, 2017 (July 13, 2017): 16-25.

Maxim Eristavi, *Why the US Keeps Losing the Fight Against Disinformation*, Atlantic Council, July 24, 2017.

Anne Applebaum, "Maybe the A.I. Dystopia Is Already Here," *Washington Post*, July 28, 2017.

Sean Illing, "China Is Perfecting A New Method for Suppressing Dissent on the Internet," *Vox*, August 2, 2017.

Jim Rutenberg, "RT, Sputnik and Russia's New Theory of War," *New York Times*, September 13, 2017.

Susan Landau, "Russia's Hybrid Warriors Got the White House. Now They're Coming for America's Town Halls," *Foreign Policy*, September 26, 2017.

Karina Orlova, "Make America Vigilant Again," *American Interest*, September 29, 2017.

Patrick M. Cronin and Harry Krejsa, "5 Ways America Can Defends Itself from 'Nonphysical' Attacks," *National Interest*, October 3, 2017.

"Baltics Battle Russia in Online Disinformation War," *Deutsche Welle*, October 8, 2017.

Reid Standish, "Russia's Neighbors Respond to Putin's 'Hybrid War,'" *Foreign Policy*, October 12, 2017.

Max Boot, "Russia Has Invented Social Media Blitzkrieg," *Foreign Policy*, October 13, 2017.

David Ignatius, "Russia Is Pushing to Control Cyberspace. We Should All Be Worried," *Washington Post*, October 24, 2017.

Patrick Tucker, "How NATO Is Preparing to Fight Tomorrow's Information Wars," *Defense One*, October 26, 2017.

Dan Lamothe, "In Finland, Mattis Backs Creation of a Hybrid Warfare Center Focused on Russia," *Washington Post*, November 6, 2017.

Citations from January 2018 through June 2018

David Ignatius, "Russia's Radical New Strategy for Information Warfare," *Washington Post*, January 18, 2018.

Reid Standish, "Inside a European Center to Combat Russia's Hybrid Warfare," *Foreign Policy*, January 18, 2018.

Ihor Kabanenko, "Russian 'Hybrid War' Tactics at Sea: Targeting Underwater Communications Cables," *Eurasia Daily Monitor*, January 23, 2018.

Joshua Stowell, "What is Hybrid Warfare?" *Global Security Review*, February 2, 2018.

Mark Pomerleau, "Why DoD Leaders Are Increasingly Worried About the 'Gray Zone,'" *C4ISRNet*, February 5, 2018.

Dan Mahaffee, "We've Lost the Opening Info Battle against Russia; Let's Not Lose the War," *Defense One*, February 23, 2018.

Max Boot, "Russia's Been Waging War on the West for Years. We Just Haven't Noticed," *Washington Post*, March 15, 2018.

Chris Meserole and Alina Polyakova, "Disinformation Wars," *Foreign Policy*, May 25, 2018.

Max Boot, "The United States Is Preparing for the Wrong War," *Washington Post*, March 29, 2018.

Giorgi Menabde, "Russia Employs New 'Hybrid War' Methods Against Georgia," *Eurasia Daily Monitor*, March 29, 2018.

Abigail Tracy, "'A Different Kind of Propaganda': Has America Lost the Information War," *Vanity Fair*, April 23, 2018.

Hal Brands, "Putin Is Playing With Fire and We All May Get Burned," *Bloomberg*, May 8, 2018.

John Grady, "Panel: U.S. Needs Non-Military Options to Handle 'Gray Zone' Warfare from Russia, China, Iran," *USNI News*, May 15, 2018.

Jed Willard, "What Europe Can Teach America About Russian Disinformation," *Atlantic*, June 9, 2018.

Janusz Bugajski, *Moscow's Anti-Western Social Offensive*, Center for European Policy Analysis (CEPA), June 13, 2018.

Sydney J. Freedberg Jr., "Russia, China Are Outmaneuvering US: Generals Recommend New Authorities, Doctrine," *Breaking Defense*, June 15, 2018.

Citations from July 2018 through December 2019

Nicole Ng and Eugene Rumer, "The West Fears Russia's Hybrid Warfare. They're Missing the Bigger Picture." Carnegie Endowment for International Peace, July 3, 2019.

Joe Pappalardo, "Now NATO Says Russian 'Hybrid Warfare' Could Start a Real War," *Popular Mechanics*, July 13, 2018.

Richard A. Bitzinger, "Russia's Trump Card: Hybrid Warfare," *Asia Times*, July 18, 2018.

Nathan Freier, *The Darker Shade of Gray: A New War Unlike Any Other*, Center for Strategic and International Studies, July 27, 2018.

Stanislaw Zaryn, "Russia's Hybrid Warfare Toolkit Has More to Offer Than Propaganda," *Defense News*, August 9, 2019.

Andrew Chuter, "NATO to Define Plan to Counter Russia's Hybrid Warfare Tactics," *Defense News*, December 3, 2019.

Citations from January 2020 through December 2020

Donald Stoker and Craig Whiteside, "Blurred Lines: Gray-Zone Conflict and Hybrid War—Two Failures of American Strategic Thinking," *Naval War College Review*, Winter 2020.

Robert C. Rubel, "Canary In The Coal Mine: The US Navy's Dilemmas As An Indication Of A Culminating Point In National Grand Strategy," *Journal of Political Risk*, April 2020.

Hal Brands, "Don't Let Great Powers Carve Up the World, Spheres of Influence Are Unnecessary and Dangerous," *Foreign Affairs*, April 20, 2020.

Joshua Tallis, "To Compete With Russia and China at Sea, Think Small," *Defense One*, May 12, 2020.

Jeff Goodson, "Irregular Warfare in a New Era of Great-Power Competition," Modern War Institute, May 20, 2020.

Seth Cropsey, "Can We Keep Our 'Grey Zone' Edge Over Our Enemies?" *The Hill*, June 16, 2020.

Anthony H. Cordesman with the assistance of Grace Hwang, *Chronology of Possible Chinese Gray Area and Hybrid Warfare Operations*, CSIS, working draft, July 2, 2020, 20 pp.

Anthony H. Cordesman with the assistance of Grace Hwang, *Chronology of Possible Russian Gray Area and Hybrid Warfare Operations*, CSIS, working draft, July 2, 2020, 17 pp.

Christopher England, "How Great-Power Politics Will Be Used in an Asymmetric Era," *National Interest*, August 5, 2020.

Alexander Lott, "What Does Hybrid Warfare Mean for Maritime Security?" *National Interest*, August 9, 2020.

Anthony H. Cordesman with the assistance of Grace Hwang, *U.S. Competition with China and Russia: The Crisis-Driven Need to Change U.S. Strategy*, CSIS, working draft, August 11, 2020, 154 pp.

Jim Mitre and Andre Gellerman, "Defining DoD's Role in Gray Zone Competition," CNAS, August 24, 2020.

Eric Robinson, "The Missing, Irregular Half of Great Power Competition," Modern War Institute, September 8, 2020.

Aaron Mehta, "Irregular Warfare Strategies Must Move Beyond Special Forces, Pentagon Says," *Defense News*, October 2, 2020.

Sean McFate, "Irregular Warfare with China, Russia: Ready or Not, It's Coming—If Not Already Here," *The Hill*, October 11, 2020.

Hal Brands, "Pentagon's New Plan to Fight China and Russia in the Gray Zone," *Bloomberg*, October 21, 2020.

Elisabeth Braw, "The West Is Surprisingly Well-Equipped for Gray-Zone Deterrence," *Defense One*, October 28, 2020.

Sam Mullins, "Great Power Competition Versus Counterterrorism: A False Dichotomy," *Just Security*, October 23, 2020.

Stephen Tankel and Tommy Ross, "Retooling U.S. Security Sector Assistance," *War on the Rocks*, October 28, 2020.

Raffaello Pantucci, "Beijing Aims to Avoid Battle But Win War with New Dark Arts," *Times (UK)*, December 26, 2020.

Citations from January 2021 through June 2021

Michael J. Mazarr, Joe Cheravitch, Jeffrey W. Hornung, and Stephanie Pezard, *What Deters and Why, Applying a Framework to Assess Deterrence of Gray Zone Aggression*, RAND, 2021, 140 pp.

Kevin Bilms, "Better Understanding Irregular Warfare in Competition," *Military Times*, January 1, 2021.

Kevin Bilms, "What's in a Name? Reimagining Irregular Warfare Activities for Competition," *War on the Rocks*, January 15, 2021.

Mathieu Boulègue and Alina Polyakova, "The Evolution of Russian Hybrid Warfare: Introduction," CEPA, January 29, 2021.

Precious Chatterje-Doody, "The Evolution of Russian Hybrid Warfare: United Kingdom," CEPA, January 29, 2021.

Kalev Stoicescu, "The Evolution of Russian Hybrid Warfare: Estonia," CEPA, January 29, 2021.

Kateryna Zarembo and Sergiy Solodkyy, "The Evolution of Russian Hybrid Warfare: Ukraine," CEPA, January 29, 2021.

Justin Baumann, "Using Hybrid War Theory to Shape Future U. S. Generational Doctrine," *Small Wars Journal*, February 3, 2021.

Seth G. Jones, "The Future of Competition: U.S. Adversaries and the Growth of Irregular Warfare," CSIS, February 4, 2021.

Phil W. Reynolds, "Building Partner Capacity Is Great Power Competition: The Future of 333 Funds," *Small Wars Journal*, February 6, 2021.

Mark Voyger, "What is "Hybrid Warfare," Really?" CEPA, February 24, 2021.

Tom O'Cconnor and Naveed Jamali, "As China Gray Zone Warfare Escalates, U.S. May Stand to Lose First Shooting Battle," *Newsweek*, March 4, 2021.

Robert C. Rubel, "Whispers from Wargames about the Gray Zone," *War on the Rocks*, March 8, 2021.

Elisabeth Braw, *Producing Fear in the Enemy's Mind: How to Adapt Cold War Deterrence for Gray-Zone Aggression*, American Enterprise Institute, March 2021 (posted online March 9, 2021), 18 pp.

John A. Tirpak, "U.S. Poorly Integrates CCMDs, Hasn't Figured Out Hybrid, Hyten Says," *Air Force Magazine*, March 10, 2021. (CCMDs are U.S. regional combatant commands.)

Michael Rühle, "NATO's Unified Response to Hybrid Threats," CEPA, March 22, 2021.

Bridget Bachman, "Hybrid: An Adjective Describing the Current War," *Small Wars Journal*, March 25, 2021.

Elisabeth Braw, *Building A Wall of Denial Against Gray-Zone Aggression*, American Enterprise Institute, April 2021 (posted online April 12, 2021), 24 pp.

Adam Taylor, "Irregular Conflict in a Great Power World: A Word of Caution for the Marine Corps," *Small Wars Journal*, April 6, 2021.

David Knoll, Kevin Pollpeter, and Sam Plapinger, "China's Irregular Approach to War: The Myth of a Purely Conventional Future Fight," Modern War Institute, April 27, 2021.

Alex Hollings, "America Needs New Covert Options for Great Power Competition," *Sandboxx*, May 21, 2021.

Lesley Seebeck, "Zeroing In on the Grey Zone in the Indo-Pacific," *Strategist (ASPI)*, June 24, 2021.

Citations from July 2021 through December 2021

Peter Layton, *China's Enduring Grey-Zone Challenge*, Air and Space Power Centre (Royal Australian Air Force, Australian Department of Defence), July 2021 (posted online July 13, 2021), 97 pp.

Hal Brands, "Russian and Iranian Proxy Forces Are Baffling the U.S., Drones, Mercenaries and Cyberattacks Give Rivals Plausible Deniability for Damaging American Interests," *Bloomberg*, July 22, 2021.

Matthew Sussex, "Learning in the Grey Zone: How Democracies Can Meet the Authoritarian Challenge," *Strategist (ASPI)*, July 22, 2021.

James Holmes, "To Beat China In The Gray Zone, You Have To Be There," *19FortyFive*, July 28, 2021.

Heather A. Conley and Colin Wall, *Hybrid Threats in the Arctic: Scenarios and Policy Options in a Vulnerable Region*, European Centre of Excellence for Countering Hybrid Threats (Hybrid CoE), 7 pp. (Hybrid CoE Strategic Analysis 28, posted online August 26, 2021.)

Hall Gardner, "Why America and Europe Need a Transatlantic Strategic Council, Stronger U.S.-EU Strategic Coordination Is Urgently Needed to Prevent the Possibility that Regional Conflicts Could Draw the United States and the Europeans into New Forms of 'Hybrid Warfare' Against a Eurasian Axis of Predominantly 'Authoritarian' States," *National Interest*, August 27, 2021.

Elisabeth Braw, "Zapad-2021: Russia is Perfecting the Art of Grey-Zone Warfare, *Reaction*, September 10, 2021.

Dan Altman, "The Future of Conquest, Fights Over Small Places Could Spark the Next Big War," *Foreign Affairs*, September 24, 2021.

Ashley Townshend, Thomas Lonergan, and Toby Warden, "The U.S.-Australian Alliance Needs a Strategy to Deter China's Gray-Zone Coercion," *War on the Rocks*, September 29, 2021.

Sean M. Zeigler, Dara Massicot, Elina Treyger, Naoko Aoki, Chandler Sachs, and Stephen Watts, *Analysis of Russian Irregular Threats*, RAND, 2021, 22 pp.

Peter Layton, "Countering China's Gray Zone Strategy," *Small Wars Journal*, October 10, 2021.

Gabriel Lloyd, "Hybrid Warfare and Active Measures," *Small Wars Journal*, October 10, 2021.

Elisabeth Braw, "Countering Aggression in the Gray Zone," American Enterprise Institute, November 18, 2021.

Andrés Ortega, "All Wars Are Hybrid, but War and the Notion of Hybrid Have Changed," Real Instituto Elcano, November 30, 2021.

Danny Pronk, *Fifty Shades of Grey, 21ˢᵗ Century Strategic Competition with Russia and China*, Clingendael Institute (Netherlands Institute of International Relations), December 2021 (posted online December 2, 2021), 10 pp.

Ben Hall, Sam Fleming, and James Shotter, "How Migration Became a Weapon in a 'Hybrid War,' Governments Are Increasingly Using Displaced People to Exploit Europe's Divisions and Fears over Migrants," *Financial Times*, December 5, 2021.

Jake Harrington and Riley McCabe, *Detect and Understand, Modernizing Intelligence for the Gray Zone*, Center for Strategic and International Studies, December 2021 (posted online December 7 2021), 13 pp.

Megan Price, "Taming the 'Grey Zone,' It Has Become Something of a Catch-All Phrase. But if Everything Is a Grey Zone Tactic, to What Extent Is This Helpful?" *Interpreter*, December 7, 2021.

Brahma Chellaney, "China's Global Hybrid War," *Strategist (ASPI)*, December 10, 2021.

Sean Monaghan, "Bad Idea: Winning the Gray Zone," *Defense 360 (CSIS)*, December 17, 2021.

Max Hastings, "In Today's Wars, Everything Is a Weapon, It's Not Just Gray Zones and Putin's Little Green Men: Conflict Is Now Carried Out in Banks, Courts and Even Movie Theaters," *Bloomberg*, December 19, 2021.

Citations from January 2022

Joe Gould and Mark Pomerleau, "Why the US Should Fight Russia, China in the 'Gray Zone,'" *C4ISRNet*, January 4, 2022.

Elisabeth Braw, "Biden's Gray-Zone Gaffe Highlights a Real Dilemma, It's High Time for NATO and Its Member Governments to Define what Kinds of Aggression Short of War Require a Unified Response," *Defense One*, January 20, 2022.

Jake Harrington and Riley Mccabe, "Keeping Pace in the Gray Zone: Three Recommendations for the U.S. Intelligence Community," *War on the Rocks*, February 1, 2022.

Marc Polymeropoulos and Arun Iyer, "US Adversaries Have Been Mastering Hybrid Warfare. It's Time to Catch Up," *Atlantic Council*, February 8, 2022.

Charity S. Jacobs and Kathleen M. Carley, "Taiwan: China's Gray Zone Doctrine in Action," *Small Wars Journal*, February 11, 2022.

Forward Defense experts, "Today's Wars Are Fought in the 'Gray Zone.' Here's Everything You Need to Know about It," *Atlantic Council*, February 23, 2022.

Peter Layton, "China's Grey Zone Tactics Amount to Far More than Just Laser Games," *Interpreter,* February 25, 2022.

By Tarik Solmaz, "'Hybrid Warfare': One Term, Many Meanings," *Small Wars Journal*, February 25, 2022.

Roderick Lee and Marcus Clay, "Don't Call It a Gray Zone: China's Use-of-Force Spectrum," *War on the Rocks*, May 9, 2022.

James Holmes, "How The U.S. Navy Can Compete With China In The Gray-Zone," *19FortyFive*, November 6, 2022.

Mark Pomerleau, "In light of great power competition, DOD reevaluating irregular warfare and info ops," *Defense Scoop*, November 21, 2022.

Sean McFate, "Irregular Warfare Will Win 'Strategic Competition,'" *The Hill*, December 4, 2022.

Appendix F. Congress and the Late 1980s/Early 1990s Transition to Post–Cold War Era

This appendix provides additional background information on the role of Congress in responding to the transition in the late 1980s and early 1990s from the Cold War to the post–Cold War era.

This transition prompted a broad reassessment by DOD and Congress of defense funding levels, strategy, and missions that led to numerous changes in DOD plans and programs. Many of these changes were articulated in the 1993 Bottom-Up Review (BUR),[146] a reassessment of U.S. defense plans and programs whose very name conveyed the fundamental nature of the reexamination that had occurred.[147] In general, the BUR reshaped the U.S. military into a force that was smaller than the Cold War U.S. military, and oriented toward a planning scenario being able to conduct two major regional contingencies (MRCs) rather than the Cold War planning scenario of a NATO-Warsaw Pact conflict.[148]

Through both committee activities and the efforts of individual Members, Congress played a significant role in the reassessment of defense funding levels, strategy, plans, and programs that was prompted by the end of the Cold War. In terms of committee activities, the question of how to change U.S. defense plans and programs in response to the end of the Cold War was, for example, a major focus for the House and Senate Armed Services Committees in holding hearings and marking up annual national defense authorization acts in the early 1990s.[149]

---

[146] See Department of Defense, *Report on the Bottom-Up Review*, Les Aspin, Secretary of Defense, October 1993, 109 pp.

[147] Secretary of Defense Les Aspin's introduction to DOD's report on the 1993 BUR states

> In March 1993, I initiated a comprehensive review of the nation's defense strategy, force structure, modernization, infrastructure, and foundations. I felt that a department-wide review needed to be conducted "from the bottom up" because of the dramatic changes that have occurred in the world as a result of the end of the Cold War and the dissolution of the Soviet Union. These changes in the international security environment have fundamentally altered America's security needs. Thus, the underlying premise of the Bottom-Up Review was that we needed to reassess all of our defense concepts, plans, and programs from the ground up.
>
> (Department of Defense, *Report on the Bottom-Up Review*, Les Aspin, Secretary of Defense, October 1993, p. iii.)

[148] For additional discussion of the results of the BUR, see CRS Report 93-839 F, *Defense Department Bottom-Up Review: Results and Issues*, October 6, 1993, 6 pp., by Edward F. Bruner, and CRS Report 93-627 F, *Defense Department Bottom-Up Review: The Process*, July 2, 1993, 9 pp., by Cedric W. Tarr Jr. (both nondistributable and available to congressional clients from CRS).

[149] See, for example, the following:

> the House Armed Services Committee's report on the FY1991 National Defense Authorization Act (H.Rept. 101-665 of August 3, 1990, on H.R. 4739), pp. 7-14;
>
> the Senate Armed Services Committee's report on the FY1991 National Defense Authorization Act (S.Rept. 101-384 of July 20 (legislative day, July 10), 1990, on S. 2884), pp. 8-36;
>
> the House Armed Services Committee's report on the FY1992 and FY1993 National Defense Authorization Act (H.Rept. 102-60 of May 13, 1991, on H.R. 2100), pp. 8 and 13;
>
> the Senate Armed Services Committee's report on the FY1992 and FY1993 National Defense Authorization Act (S.Rept. 102-113 of July 19 (legislative day, July 8), 1991, on S. 1507), pp. 8-9;
>
> the House Armed Services Committee's report on the FY1993 National Defense Authorization Act (H.Rept. 102-527 of May 19, 1992, on H.R. 5006), pp. 8-10, 14-15, and 22;
>
> the Senate Armed Services Committee's report on the FY1993 National Defense Authorization Act (S.Rept. 102-352 of July 31 (legislative day, July 23), 1992, on S. 3114), pp. 7-12;

(continued...)

In terms of efforts by individual Members, some Members put forth their own proposals for how much to reduce defense spending from the levels of the final years of the Cold War,[150] while others put forth detailed proposals for future U.S. defense strategy, plans, programs, and spending. Senator John McCain, for example, issued a detailed, 32-page policy paper in November 1991 presenting his proposals for defense spending, missions, force structure, and weapon acquisition programs.[151]

Perhaps the most extensive individual effort by a Member to participate in the reassessment of U.S. defense following the end of the Cold War was the one carried out by Representative Les Aspin, the chairman of the House Armed Services Committee. In early 1992, Aspin, supported by members of the committee's staff, devised a force-planning standard and potential force levels and associated defense spending levels U.S. defense for the new post–Cold War era. A principal aim of Aspin's effort was to create an alternative to the "Base Force" plan for U.S. defense in the post–Cold War era that had been developed by the George H. W. Bush Administration.[152] Aspin's effort included a series of policy papers in January and February 1992[153] that were augmented by press releases and speeches. Aspin's policy paper of February 25, 1992, served as the basis for his testimony that same day at a hearing on future defense spending before the House Budget Committee. Although DOD and some other observers (including some Members of Congress)

---

the House Armed Services Committee's report on the FY1994 National Defense Authorization Act (H.Rept. 103-200 of July 30, 1993, on H.R. 2401), pp. 8-9 and 18-19;

the House Armed Services Committee's report on the FY1995 National Defense Authorization Act (H.Rept. 103-499 of May 10, 1994, on H.R. 4301), pp. 7 and 9;

the Senate Armed Services Committee's report on the FY1995 National Defense Authorization Act (S.Rept. 103-282 of June 14 (legislative day, June 7), 1994, on S. 2182), pp. 8-9; and

the House Armed Services Committee's report on the FY1996 National Defense Authorization Act (H.Rept. 104-131 of June 1, 1995, on H.R. 1530), pp. 6-7 and 11-12.

[150] See, for example, Clifford Krauss, "New Proposal for Military Cut," *New York Times*, January 7, 1992: A11 (discussing a proposal by Senator Phil Gramm for reducing defense spending by a certain amount); "Sen. Mitchell Proposes $100 Billion Cut in Defense," *Aerospace Daily*, January 17, 1992: 87; John Lancaster, "Nunn Proposes 5-Year Defense Cut of $85 Billion," *Washington Post*, March 25, 1992: A4.

[151] Senator John McCain, Matching A Peace Dividend With National Security, A New Strategy For The 1990s, November 1991, 32 pp.

[152] See, for example, "Arms Panel Chief Challenges Ending Use of Threat Analysis," *Aviation Week & Space Technology*, January 13, 1992: 28; Patrick E. Tyler, "Top Congressman Seeks Deeper Cuts in Military Budget," *New York Times*, February 23, 1991: 1; Barton Gellman, "Debate on Military's Future Crystallizes Around 'Enemies List,'" *Washington Post*, February 26, 1992: A20; Pat Towell, "Planning the Nation's Defense," *CQ*, February 29, 1992: 479. For more on the Base Force, see CRS Report 92-493 S, *National Military Strategy, The DoD Base Force, and U.S. Unified Command Plan*, June 11, 1992, 68 pp., by John M. Collins (nondistributable and available to congressional clients from CRS).

[153] These policy papers included the following:

- National Security in the 1990s: Defining a New Basis for U.S. Military Forces, Representative Les Aspin, Chairman, House Armed Services Committee, Before the Atlantic Council of the United States, January 6, 1992, 23 pp.;

- An Approach to Sizing American Conventional Forces For the Post-Soviet Era, Representative Les Aspin, Chairman, House Armed Services Committee, January 24, 2991, 20 pp.;

- Tomorrow's Defense From Today's Industrial Base: Finding the Right Resource Strategy For A New Era, by Representative Les Aspin, Chairman, House Armed Services Committee, Before the American Defense Preparedness Association, February 12, 1992, 20 pp.; and

- An Approach to Sizing American Conventional Forces For the Post-Soviet Era, Four Illustrative Options, Representative Les Aspin, Chairman, House Armed Services Committee, February 25, 1992, 27 pp.

criticized Aspin's analysis and proposals on various grounds,[154] the effort arguably proved consequential the following year, when Aspin became Secretary of Defense in the new Clinton Administration. Aspin's 1992 effort helped inform his participation in DOD's 1993 BUR. The 1993 BUR in turn created a precedent for the subsequent Quadrennial Defense Review (QDR) process (renamed Defense Strategy Review in 2015) that remained in place until 2016.

Author Information

Ronald O'Rourke
Specialist in Naval Affairs

Disclaimer

---

[154] See, for example, "Aspin Defense Budget Plans Rebuffed By Committee," *Defense Daily*, February 24, 1992: 289; "Pentagon Spurns Aspin's Budget Cuts as 'Political,'" *Washington Post*, February 28, 1992: A14.